ENVIRONMENTAL PROTECTION AND SUSTAINABLE DEVELOPMENT

LEGAL PRINCIPLES AND RECOMMENDATIONS

ENVIRONMENTAL PROTECTION
AND SUSTAINABLE DEVELOPMENT
LEGAL PRINCIPLES AND RECOMMENDATIONS

adopted by the

**EXPERTS GROUP ON ENVIRONMENTAL LAW
OF THE WORLD COMMISSION
ON ENVIRONMENT AND DEVELOPMENT**

R. D. MUNRO, Chairman   J. G. LAMMERS, Rapporteur

JUNE 1986

with a foreword by

NAGENDRA SINGH
PRESIDENT OF THE
INTERNATIONAL COURT OF JUSTICE

Graham & Trotman / Martinus Nijhoff
Members of the Kluwer Academic Publishers Group
LONDON/DORDRECHT/BOSTON

First published in 1987 by
Graham & Trotman Limited
Sterling House
66 Wilton Road
London SW1V 1DE

Graham & Trotman
Kluwer Academic
  Publishers Group
101 Philip Drive
Assinippi Park
Norwell, MA 02061
USA

British Library Cataloguing in Publication Data
Legal principles and recommendations for
    environmental protection and sustainable
    development.
    1. Environmental law, International
    I. Experts Group on Environmental Law
    341.7′62   K3585.4

Library of Congress Cataloging-in-Publication Data
Environmental protection and sustainable development.
    1. Environmental law, International.   I. Munro, R. D.
    II. Lammers, J. G.   III. World Commission on Environment
    and Development. Experts Group on Environmental law.
    K3585.4.E585   1987   341.7′62   87-12232

ISBN 0−86010−910−0

Typeset by Acorn Bookwork, Salisbury, Wiltshire
Printed and bound in Great Britain at the Alden Press, Oxford

CONTENTS

FOREWORD

BY H. E. JUDGE NAGENDRA SINGH*

President, International Court of Justice
Member, World Commission on Environment and Development
Fellow of the British Academy; Chancellor of the University of Goa

This important innovative report of the Experts Group on Environmental Law which was established by the World Commission on Environment and Development, must be seen within the context of rapidly accelerating ecological and economic interdependence and of the work of the World Commission which recently reported on its review** of development issues and on prospects for sustainable development at national and international level.

New Imperatives for Co-operation among Nations and International Law

National boundaries are now so very permeable that traditional distinctions between local, national, and international issues have become blurred. Policies formerly considered to be exclusively matters of "national concern" now have an impact on the ecological basis of other nations' development and survival. Conversely, the way in which the policies of certain nations— including economic, trade, monetary, and most sectoral policies—are increasingly tending to reach into the "sovereign" territory of other nations, serves to limit those nations' options in devising national solutions to their "own" problems. This fast-changing context for national action has intro-

*M.A., LL.D. (Cantab); M.A., B.Litt., LL.D. (Dublin); D.Sc. (Law) Moscow; D.C.L. (Delhi); D.L. (Peking); Barrister-at-Law; Honorary Master of the Bench, Grays Inn, London and Inns of Court Dublin; Fellow, St. John's College, Cambridge; Member of the Institute of International Law; Member of the Permanent Court of Arbitration, The Hague; Vice-President International Law Commission 1969; President of UN Commission on International Trade Law (INCITRAL) 1971.
**See World Commission on Environment and Development, *Our Common Future* (London: Oxford University Press, 1987).

duced new imperatives and new opportunities for international co-operation—and for international law.

The international legal framework needs to be significantly strengthened in support of sustainable development. Although international law relating to the environment has evolved rapidly since the 1972 Stockholm Conference on the Human Environment, there are still major gaps and deficiencies that must be overcome as part of the transition to sustainable development. A great deal of the evidence and conclusions presented in the report of the World Commission on Environment and Development calls into question the desirability—or even the feasibility—of maintaining an international system that cannot prevent one or more States from damaging the ecological basis for development and the very prospects for survival of other—or, possibly, all—States.

Both municipal and international law have too frequently lagged behind events. Today, legal regimes are being rapidly outdistanced by the accelerating pace and expanding scale of actions affecting the environmental base of development. Human laws must be reformulated to keep human activities in harmony with the unchanging and universal laws of nature. There is at the present time an urgent need:

- to strengthen and extend the application of existing laws and international agreements in support of sustainable development;
- to recognize and respect the reciprocal rights and responsibilities of individuals and States regarding sustainable development, and to apply new norms for State and interstate behaviour to enable this to be achieved;
- to reinforce existing methods and develop new procedures for avoiding and resolving disputes on environmental and resource management issues.

The report of the World Commission addresses all of these central issues of such consequence to our common future, and contains the Commission's main recommendations for essential changes in the legal framework and process, both municipal and international.

These recommendations are based on the earlier work and report of the WCED Experts Group on Environmental Law. While there are many wide-ranging proposals contained in the Legal Experts Group report, I would particularly like to highlight briefly the main principles, rights and responsibilities which require formal recognition and implementation in support of sustainable development, both within, and between, individual nations and in the international community as a whole. These main principles, rights and responsibilities are dealt with first under Section I of this Foreword.

The problem of dispute settlement in the context of the law which stands without sanctions is dealt with in Section II.

Moreover, it would be appropriate to review somewhat more elaborately the concept of extraterritorial areas as international commons and to identify some of these areas which is attempted in Section III.

I   Legal Principles, Rights and Responsibilities for Sustainable Development

The Concept of Sustainable Development

The right to development does, however, have certain limitations inasmuch as it cannot be asserted at the expense of the community or even at the expense of neighbouring States whose prospects may be jeopardized. For example a State cannot, in the name of development, proceed to applications of nuclear energy in such a way as to harm the environment and imperil human life, whether in the immediate neighbourhood or in the surrounding region. In fact, environment and development go together and have to be examined simultaneously in this context. In the process of advocating sustainable development, one has to examine the rights and responsibilities of States, both bilaterally and in relation to the international community as a whole. The need for co-operation among nations has to be viewed in the light of new imperatives. The efforts of the World Commission need to be briefly mentioned here because it makes a major contribution to the concept of development in relation to sustainability. The Commission's emphasis on "Sustainable Development" is vital to the well-being of humanity not only today but in the context of the future generations. This aspect deserves to be fully appreciated not only in the legal domain but in terms of the physical world and its prosperity on which must depend the future of humanity.

The Principles of Regulation

The general principles concerning natural resources and environmental interferences recommended by the WCED Legal Experts Group (Articles 1–8) have in common that they are applicable to *all* instances of the use of a natural resource or of an environmental interference in *any* part of the world. It follows that these general principles do not merely apply in *areas beyond the limits of national jurisdiction* or in *the transboundary context*, but also in *the entirely domestic domain*, an area which, according to traditional international

law, is subject to the exclusive jurisdiction of States. Such principles
accordingly purport, as it were, to break open traditional international law
concerning the use of natural resources or environmental interferences.

The first general principle proposed by the Legal Experts Group of the
WCED is the fundamental human right of all human beings to an environment adequate for their health and well-being. Even though this right is not
yet well-established under present international law, it certainly deserves to
be promoted with all possible vigour.

The scope of the recommendations made by the Legal Experts Group must
not be confined to the needs of the present-day world population and Article
2 accordingly provides that States shall ensure that the environment and
natural resources are conserved and used for the benefit of present *and future*
generations. This basic obligation is further elaborated by the WCED Legal
Experts Group in a number of additional articles.

For example, States must maintain ecosystems and related ecological
processes essential for the functioning of the biosphere in all its variety. They
must maintain maximum biological diversity and observe, in the exploitation of living national resources and ecosystems, the principle of *optimum*
sustainable yield (Article 3). The latter principle means that living natural
resources or ecosystems must only be utilized in such a manner and to such an
extent that benefits from those resources will be made available indefinitely.
If this principle is not obeyed the resource will diminish or may even be
extinguished. It follows that, by promoting the principle of *optimum* sustainable use, the Legal Experts Group of the WCED goes beyond the concept of
maximum sustainable yield which, as scientific analyses have indicated, still
entails severe risks of stock depletion as it makes no allowance for a margin of
error, lack of adequate data and/or uncertainty.

In order to meet this requirement to ensure that the environment and
natural resources are conserved and used for the benefit of present and future
generations, there is a need for more auxiliary action of a procedural and/or
technical nature. For example, States are to establish specific environmental
standards and both collect and disseminate data concerning natural resources
and the environment (Article 4). States shall further make or require
environmental impact assessments before carrying out or permitting
activities which may significantly affect a natural resource or the environment
(Article 5). They shall also inform all persons in a timely manner of activities
which may significantly affect their use of a natural resource or their
environment and shall grant those persons access to and due process in
administrative and judicial proceedings (Article 6). States shall, in addition,
ensure that the conservation of natural resources and the environment is

treated as an *integral part* of the planning and implementation of development activities (Article 7). In the fulfilment of all their obligations States shall, moreover, *co-operate* in good faith with other States or through competent international organizations (Article 8).

The Legal Experts Group of the WCED rightly feels the need to formulate, in addition to these principles of general application, other principles *specifically* concerning *transboundary* natural resources and environmental interferences (Articles 9–20). Indeed, the juxtaposition of sovereign States in present international law entails, in the transboundary context, certain special problems needing to be dealt with by the application of special norms.

One of these norms is that transboundary natural resources are to be used in a reasonable and equitable manner (Article 9). The international law regarding the waters of an international watercourse has considerably developed since the days of US Attorney-General Harmon (who in 1895 claimed an absolute right of the United States to dispose of the waters in its territory) and this development may now be taken to relate not only to international watercourses, but to *all* transboundary natural resources.

While the above-mentioned norm relates to the *use* of a transboundary natural resource, another substantive norm provides that States must, in principle, prevent or abate any transboundary *environmental interference* or significant risk thereof which may give rise to substantial harm (Article 10).

It is most interesting to see to what extent this basic substantive principle—which may be deemed to be generally accepted—has been qualified by the Legal Experts Group of the WCED.

In the first place, the Legal Experts Group proposes—even when this basic norm is not breached (e.g. when there is no question of *substantial* harm or of a *significant* risk)—that States should be obligated not to discriminate between the external and internal detrimental effects of activities planned and carried out in their territory (Article 13).

Article 11 is, moreover, of major interest in view of the steady increase in ultrahazardous activities and the incidents to which these activities may give rise (e.g. Bhopal, Chernobyl, and the chemical pollution of the Rhine caused by the Swiss Sandoz company). This article authorizes such ultrahazardous activities under certain conditions, but at the same time stipulates that *compensation shall be paid* should substantial harm occur in the territory of another State or in an area beyond the limits of national jurisdiction. The WCED Legal Experts Group is then clearly in favour of strict liability for the injurious consequences occasioned by certain activities even though not prohibited by international law. They propose, moreover, a special procedure in cases where a State is planning to carry out or permit an activity which will *definitely* entail a transboundary environmental interference causing harm which is substantial, albeit far less substantial than the overall technical and socio-economic cost or loss of benefits involved in preventing or reducing an interference of the kind envisaged. Such a State would enter into negotiations with the affected State, in order to determine the equitable conditions under which the activity could be carried out (Article 12).

In addition to the above-mentioned principles of a relatively *substantive* nature, the WCED Legal Experts Group proposes a number of principles concerning *co-operation* between States to implement the substantive principles. At a time of growing scarcity of natural resources and increasing deterioration of the environment, it is cause for rejoicing that the WCED Legal Experts Group should recommend (in Article 14) that co-operation shall, as much as possible, be aimed at arriving at an *optimal* use of the transboundary natural resource or at *maximizing* the effectiveness of measures to prevent or abate a transboundary environmental interference.

The general duty to co-operate is elaborated in more specific obligations concerning the exchange of information (Article 15); prior notice of planned activities and environmental impact assessments (Article 16); consultations (Article 17); co-operative arrangements for environmental assessment and protection (Article 18); and emergency situations (Article 19).

Apart from obligations imposed on States and designed to govern their relationships *inter se*, the WCED Legal Experts Group also—and quite rightly—wishes to strengthen the legal position of private persons who have been or may be detrimentally affected by a transboundary interference with their use of a transboundary natural resource or by a transboundary environmental interference. States shall provide such persons with equal access as well as due process and equal treatment in the same administrative and judicial proceedings as are available to persons within their own jurisdiction who have been or may be similarly affected (Article 20).

II   *The Problem of Dispute Settlement in Relation to the Law Without Sanctions*

The WCED Legal Experts Group finally proposes two articles which are intended to supplement *all* those mentioned previously. The first of these, namely Article 21, restates the responsibility of a State under international law for a breach of an international obligation relating to the use of a natural resource or the prevention or abatement of an environmental interference. The second, namely Article 22, relates to the peaceful settlement of environmental disputes. Here the WCED Legal Experts Group proposes a step-by-step approach to the settlement of such disputes, and provides that a State may unilaterally resort to arbitral or judicial settlement in cases in which non-binding peaceful means (particularly conciliation) do not lead to a settlement of the dispute within a certain period of time.

The new procedure proposed in Article 22 raises the possibility of invoking a binding process of dispute settlement at the request of any State. Although binding settlement is not the preferred method for settling international disputes, such a provision is now needed—not only as a last resort to avoid prolonged disputes and possible serious environmental damage, but also to encourage and provide an incentive for all parties to reach agreement within a reasonable time on either a solution or a mutually acceptable means, such as mediation, whereby a solution may be sought.

It is common knowledge that international law is currently required to confront the demands for legal regulation of problems in an international environment in which the political commitment of States, and other entities, is inadequate. One must unhesitatingly face the fact that in the background of international economic development and even in other cognate fields, the requisite effective political will is still lacking. The absence of that will, or what one may describe as the unbending character of the sovereign will, to respond to the call of the rule of law, is imposing an undue if not impossible burden upon international law in its quest for a progressive development of international economic law and regulation in allied fields. This reality, however unpleasant it may be, has to be appreciated—not only by those formulating the right to sustained development, but also by those concerned in its implementation. May I submit, therefore, that the burning question now confronting jurists in their exercise towards promoting the well-being of the law, concerns the prevailing political framework which displays a totally inadequate political commitment to any regime of regulation other than one based on reciprocal advantage? The result is that regulation can be easily formulated, but cannot be translated into enforceable law. The crucial problem is to bring about a crystallization of international co-operation into the field of enforceable law—an aspect calling for a great deal more than efforts solely directed towards the formulation of new laws or rights without any method or machinery to enforce them. *"Ubi jus ibi remedium"*—if there is a right there should be a remedy. However, in the domain of interstate law, rights are recognized in solemn treaties like the UN Charter—but the remedy remains a distant cry. Surely this aspect needs greater attention for the well-being of that law, and should be given priority over any other consideration. The WCED Legal Experts Group has therefore thought wise to recommend at least a compulsory procedure for settling disputes without directly proposing compelling adjudication since approach to the courts of law by sovereign States is not very popular. If compulsory jurisdiction of a tribunal for settling environmental disputes is to be dreaded surely the peaceful procedural compulsion to reach solutions should be acceptable. In that context the procedural concept proposed in Article 22 by the WCED Legal Experts Group should receive immediate and serious consideration by States and become established practice as soon as possible.

On this aspect of the matter I consider it necessary to strongly support the WCED's recommendation regarding the strengthening of the existing machinery for dispute settlement provided by the two international institutions functioning in the Peace Palace at The Hague, the Netherlands. The first is the International Court of Justice and the other is the Permanent Court of Arbitration. They both stand for dispute settlement by peaceful means invoking the rule of law. The recommendation of the WCED on this aspect is as follows:

> The capabilities of the Permanent Court of Arbitration and the International Court of Justice to deal with environmental and resource management problems also should be strengthened. And States should consider making greater use of the World Court's capacity under Article 26 of its Statute to form special chambers for dealing with particular cases or categories of cases, including environmental protection or resource management cases. The Court has declared its willingness and readiness to deal with such cases fully and promptly.

It is indeed gratifying to note here that the International Court of Justice has observed recently that its doors are always open to welcome consideration of any request for settlement of environmental disputes by invoking either the special chamber of jurisdiction of the Court or adjudication by the whole Court, whichever method the parties preferred. To highlight that attitude of the World Court I quote the exact words used by the Court in its report to the General Assembly in 1986, which ran as follows:

> 14. One of the questions considered by the Court, relating to the organization of its judicial work, was the possibility of constituting a chamber for the purpose of dealing with cases concerning problems of the environment. The Court took the view that it was not necessary to set up a standing special chamber, but emphasized that it was able to respond rapidly to requests for the constitution, pursuant to Article 26, Paragraph 2, of the Statute, of a special chamber to which any case, and therefore any environmental case, could be submitted. (Report of the International

Court of Justice, General Assembly, Forty-First Session, Supplement No. 4 (A/41/4)).

Furthermore, the Permanent Court of Arbitration will also welcome the idea of maintaining an additional list of experts, both legal and scientific specialists on the subject of environment for the purpose of helping settlement of environmental disputes by the method of arbitration if the parties chose to select that method. The aforesaid proposal to make full use of the existing international machinery for peaceful judicial settlement to include environmental disputes as well are to be welcomed and merit a mention in the present context.

III   Development and the Concept of "Extraterritorial" Areas as "International Commons" and Their Identification

The territorial jurisdiction of the nation State—whether on land, sea or air—is for the most part well established and well-known. Modern technology has opened up areas beyond the traditional terrestrial jurisdiction of States, and is even now continuing to do so. These areas are often described as "international commons" or "extraterritorial spaces" and they are becoming a growing field for the development of international law.

The concept of the *high seas*, as an international highway for the passage of merchant ships, was the first to be developed as a common space beyond the territorial sovereignty of any nation State. It is noteworthy that, for the high seas and the sea-bed outside the limits of national jurisdiction, a legal regime exists in the 1982 Law of the Sea Convention, yet that regime is not yet in full operation as the convention has yet to come into force.

There are other extraterritorial spaces, such as *outer space* or the *environment* in general, which are neither fully nor effectively covered by an up-to-date legal system. The most recent efforts are those of the environmentalists who are attempting to secure the protection, care and conservation of the *atmosphere* as a "common heritage of mankind", while nation States are busy probing *outer space* for political and strategic reasons, as well as for economic motives of exploitation.

Again the *moon* is the only celestial body that could conceivably become accessible for exploitation in the foreseeable future, and could therefore be regarded as another factor in the concept of international commons. It is now governed by the 1967 Outer Space Treaty and also by the Moon Agreement of 1979. Besides repeating the provisions of the Outer Space Treaty, the more recent Moon Agreement states that "due regard shall be paid to the interests of present and future generations as well as to the need to promote higher standards of living and conditions of economic and social progress and development" (Article 4) and also that measures be taken "to prevent the disruption of the existing balance of its environment" (Article 7). However, in its most important innovation, the agreement proclaims that "the moon and its natural resources are the common heritage of mankind" and goes on to provide for the establishment of "an international regime . . . to govern the exploitation of the natural resources of the moon", the purposes of which include "an equitable sharing by all States Parties in the benefits derived from those resources" (Article 11). As is noted above with respect to the 1982 Law of the Sea Convention, the notion of a common heritage of mankind, coupled with provisions for equitable sharing by all parties, seems to be unacceptable to any major power.

Furthermore, co-existent with outer space and the atmospheric, biospheric and inorganic terrestrial environments, there is a fifth environment which, although normally invisible to the human eye, has a growing influence on human welfare. This is another result of advances in technology and it is known as the *"electromagnetic environment"*, which surrounds the earth, permeates the atmosphere and is a phenomenon of the terrestrial planet itself. Of particular concern are (a) the communication portion of the electromagnetic spectrum (frequency range, circa $10 \times 10^3 - 300 \times 10^0$ hertz) and (b) the geostationary (geosynchronous) satellite orbit (in the equatorial plane at an altitude of circa 36,000 kilometres). It could be regarded as a special feature of the environment of radiant energy, including cosmic radiation, which envelops the earth. As of today, mankind's principal use of the electromagnetic environment is in the field of communications. An international organization, the International Telecommunication Union (ITU), has been created to facilitate international co-operation to this end. In a world which is increasingly connected and automated by means of electronics, major fluctuations in the electromagnetic environment may have serious international consequences, particularly during times of diplomatic or military crises.

Another, if quite different, area of "extraterritorial space" may be said to be the *Antarctic* continent, which has been regulated by a group of States under the 1959 Antarctic Treaty.

It is quite possible that modern technology may open up other extraterritorial elements in years to come, making it imperative to regulate these newly discovered fields if mankind is to be prevented from annihilating itself and even destroying the world. Legal regulation in this new domain is, then, vital for human well-being and prosperity—or even the very survival of

mankind. This opens a new chapter of international law, with the establishment of legal regimes in hitherto unexplored domains.

Why a Legal Regime is Needed for "Extraterritorial Spaces"

In sum, therefore, for reasons of a political or security nature, such as
defence, or of an economic nature, such as the quest for scarce resources
(including communications positioning) or by reason of the environmental
safety of mankind, there is a growing and pressing need for the proper
regulation of newly identified extraterritorial spaces. This need arises for
several reasons, of which the most noteworthy may be summarized as follows:
First, without proper regulation, the increasing competition among States
and groups of States for economic resources and for control and supremacy
over strategic positions in space could easily lead to unrestrained rivalry and
consequent instability, or indeed open conflict. *Second*, mankind's shared
anxiety for the right of present and future generations to protection, in their
interest, of the *res communis humanitatis* (common heritage of mankind). This
is a relatively new concept which has succeeded the *terra nullius*. It owes its
origins to twentieth century technology and to the realization that certain
areas, not subject to effective occupation by any single State or group of
States, nevertheless contain significant resources of value to mankind.

However, there is no real measure of agreement on how much of
extraterritorial space in fact has the status of a part of the common heritage of
mankind. Under the Law of the Sea Convention, the sea-bed and ocean floor
beyond national jurisdiction have this status, and the convention provides an
elaborate regime to administer the potential mineral wealth of the area by
means of a joint Authority and Enterprise. This regime, with its provisions
for the development of international resources and the transfer of technology
to enable developing States to obtain an equitable share of these resources in
future, may perhaps come to be a model for legal regimes to govern other
extraterritorial areas. The convention must, however, be in force and its
provisions in operation if there is to be sufficient international confidence for
States and groups of States to seek to emulate it for the regulation of other
areas such as, for example, the geostationary orbit or Antarctica. It may be
mentioned here that the report of the World Commission on Environment
and Development contains a number of observations on Antarctica, included
in the hope of enlisting the co-operation of the international community as a
whole. The Commission's concern has been to give paramountcy to the
environmental interests of that region. This environmental aspect is far more

important than the concept of a common heritage of mankind which has been objected to by some of the great powers. However, according to any basic principle regulating the environmental relations of nation States, the primacy of the environmental factor in the "international commons" as such has to be acknowledged as a matter of vital importance to the community and recognized as a *conditio sine qua non* for the health of humanity.

Suggestions for Implementation; The Next Step

The World Commission has recommended that the General Assembly commit itself to preparing a Universal Declaration and later a Convention on Environmental Protection and Sustainable Development. It has proposed that a special negotiating group could be established to draw up a draft Declaration for adoption in 1988. Once that text was approved, that group could then proceed to prepare a Convention, based on and extending the principles in the Declaration, with the aim of having an approved draft Convention ready for signature by States within three to five years. To facilitate the early inception of that process, the Commission has submitted for consideration by the General Assembly, and as a starting point for the deliberations of the special negotiating group, a number of proposed legal principles embodied in the 22 Articles put forward by the Legal Experts Group of the WCED.

Time and tide wait for no man. The sands of life are passing away swiftly and if man does not heed the warnings given by nature he will not only put an end to his very existence, but will destroy all life on earth. Immediate action is necessary to save humanity from the environmental peril created by our own neglect of nature—and this warning cannot be allowed to go unheeded.

*   *   *

The aforesaid 22 Articles are reproduced in this volume and published by the enterprising Dutch publishing house Martinus Nijhoff, with the promptness and efficiency of Mr. Stephens (publisher at Martinus Nijhoff), who has not only accepted the need but encouraged this effort at publicizing the labours of the Legal Experts Group whose concrete formulations I have had the privilege of not only witnessing but also fully appreciating as a Member of the Commission. A word of praise to the publishers is very much warranted in this case.

I could not conclude this Foreword without a word of admiration for the efforts of Mr. R. D. Munro and Dr. J. G. Lammers, who brought together and led the work of the team of top international legal experts. Those experts, and others who have contributed to this joint international effort, have rendered a service to present and future generations by setting out a new and necessary legal foundation for the protection and sustainable use of the ecological basis for human life and progress on our small planet.

CHAIRMAN'S INTRODUCTION

The Experts Group on Environmental Law was established in 1985 to prepare a report on legal principles for environmental protection and sustainable development, and proposals for accelerating the development of relevant international law, for consideration by the World Commission on Environment and Development.

The main guidelines for the work of the Experts Group were:

- to reinforce existing legal principles and to formulate new principles and rules of law which reflect and support the mainly anticipatory and preventive strategies which the Commission is committed to developing;
- to complement and build on the relevant work of other international organizations (e.g. of UNEP, the International Law Commission, The Institute of International Law, the International Law Association, IUCN, etc.);
- to give special attention to *legal principles and rules which ought to be in place now or before the year 2000* to support environmental protection and sustainable development within and among all States;
- to consider not only principles regarding the obligations of States to reduce or avoid activities affecting the environment of other States, but also principles regarding the individual and collective responsibilities of States concerning future generations, other species and ecosystems of international significance and the global commons;
- to prepare proposals for strengthening the legal and institutional framework for accelerating the development and application of international law in support of environmental protection and sustainable development within and among all States.

The Experts Group met twice, during 4–5 June 1985 and 18–20 June 1986. Both meetings were held at The Peace Palace in The Hague, with facilities and support services kindly provided by The Carnegie Foundation.

Soon after the first meeting of the Experts Group the Rapporteur Dr. Johan G. Lammers prepared a preliminary set of draft principles which were

1

circulated to the members for comment. That draft was then revised and re-circulated for comment in September 1985.

Two discussion papers on "Legal Principles for Environmental Protection and Sustainable Development" and on "The Settlement of Environmental Disputes: A Forward Look" were prepared for and discussed at the fourth meeting of the World Commission held in Sao Paulo in late October 1985.

A further draft of the "Legal Principles for Environmental Protection and Sustainable Development" was then prepared and sent in early 1986 to the Experts Group members for comment. It was subsequently revised and became the main document for discussion at the second meeting. For that meeting there were also a series of background papers with proposals for strengthening the legal and institutional framework for accelerating the development and application of relevant international law. Of special interest and merit were the "Proposals for International Environmental Law Developments Towards the Year 2000" submitted on behalf of the IUCN Commission on Environmental Policy, Law and Administration.

The proposed "Legal Principles" may be deemed to provide elements for a Draft Convention on Environmental Protection and Sustainable Development. They are laid down in 22 Articles in four distinct parts: General Principles concerning Natural Resources and Environmental Interferences (Articles 1–8); Principles Specifically concerning Transboundary Natural Resources and Environmental Interferences (Articles 9–20); State Responsibility (Article 21); and Peaceful Settlement of Disputes (Article 22).

The text of every article was approved by the members of the Experts Group, with the exception of Dr. Timoshenko as he was unfortunately unable to attend either meeting of the Experts Group, but did provide comments and suggestions which were taken into account in the various drafts and development of the proposed legal principles. The texts in the "Comment" for each article were generally agreed to by the participants at the second meeting, but time did not permit either full review or endorsement in detail of them.

The Experts Group at its second meeting also developed and agreed to a relevant set of recommendations for strengthening the legal framework and institutional arrangements for environmental protection and sustainable development.

The Experts Group was able to accomplish so much in so short a time in large part because of the dedicated and formidable work of the Rapporteur, Dr. Johan G. Lammers. He persevered under difficult circumstances and time constraints to formulate and refine many key principles, and to prepare well-researched and detailed explanatory notes for each. Also, the discussions at the two meetings were necessarily both extensive and intensive, and were only able to reach a successful conclusion through the shared knowledge and active participation and co-operation of every member of the Experts Group.

The Government of the Netherlands deserves special thanks for its constant and generous support for the work of the Experts Group, including their agreement to allow Dr. Lammers to serve as the Group's Rapporteur on part-time secondment from the Ministry of Foreign Affairs. Also, the costs of the Group's second meeting were covered by a special grant jointly from the Netherlands Ministry of Development Co-operation and the Ministry of Housing, Physical Planning and Environment.

The work of the Experts Group was inspired and driven throughout by the shared conviction of the members that there must be an accelerated development of national and international law in support of environmental protection and sustainable development within and among all countries. This report is their contribution to help launch that necessary process.

R. D. Munro
Chairman
Experts Group on Environmental Law

MEMBERS OF THE EXPERTS GROUP ON ENVIRONMENTAL LAW

Chairman:
MR. ROBERT MUNRO
Special Adviser
World Commission on Environment and
Development
Nairobi, Kenya

DR. ANDRONICO ADEDE
Director, Legal Division
International Atomic Energy Agency
Vienna, Austria

DR. FRANÇOISE BURHENNE
Head, International Law Centre
International Union for Conservation of
Nature and Natural Resources
Bonn, Federal Republic of Germany

DR. ALEXANDRE-CHARLES KISS
President of the European Council on
Environmental Law and Secretary-General of
the International Institute of Human Rights
Strasbourg, France

DR. STEPHEN McCAFFREY
Professor of Law
McGeorge School of Law
University of the Pacific
Sacramento, California, USA

DR. AKIO MORISHIMA
Professor of Law
Faculty of Law
Nagoya University
Nagoya, Japan

Rapporteur:
DR. JOHAN G. LAMMERS
Office of the Legal Adviser
Ministry of Foreign Affairs
The Hague, Netherlands

DR. ZAKI MUSTAFA
Secretary-General of the Saudi-Sudanese
Commission for the Development of Red Sea
Resources
Jeddah, Saudi Arabia

DR. HENRI SMETS
Environment Directorate
Organization for Economic Co-operation and
Development
Paris, France

MR. ROBERT STEIN
President
Environmental Mediation International
Washington, DC, USA

DR. ALBERTO SZEKELY
Chief Legal Adviser
Secretaria de Relaciones Exteriores
Mexico DF, Mexico

MR. ALEXANDRE TIMOSHENKO
Senior Scientific Worker
Institute of State and Law
Academy of Sciences of the USSR
Moscow, USSR

DR. AMADO TOLENTINO
National Environmental Protection Council
Quezon City, Philippines

4

STRENGTHENING THE LEGAL AND INSTITUTIONAL FRAMEWORK FOR ENVIRONMENTAL PROTECTION AND SUSTAINABLE DEVELOPMENT

CONSOLIDATED REPORT OF THE EXPERTS GROUP ON ENVIRONMENTAL LAW TO THE WORLD COMMISSION ON ENVIRONMENT AND DEVELOPMENT

August 1986

CONTENTS

LEGAL PRINCIPLES FOR ENVIRONMENTAL PROTECTION AND SUSTAINABLE DEVELOPMENT

The main mandate of the Experts Group was to prepare legal principles which *ought to be in place now or before the year 2000* to support environmental protection and sustainable development within and among all States.

1. Character and Structure of the Proposed Legal Principles

The proposed legal principles are developed in 22 articles which are divided into four parts dealing respectively with:

Part I   General Principles concerning Natural Resources and Environmental Interferences (Articles 1–8);

Part II   Principles Specifically concerning Transboundary Natural Resources and Environmental Interferences (Articles 9–20);

Part III   State Responsibility (Article 21);

Part IV   Peaceful Settlement of Disputes (Article 22).

The first and keystone principle is the fundamental right of all human beings to an environment adequate for their health and well-being (Article 1). The subsequent 21 articles represent key principles which need to be adopted and applied by all States individually and collectively in order to achieve sustainable development on a world-wide basis within and among all countries. The articles are presented as formal and binding obligations of and among all States. This binding character is represented in the text of the articles by the use throughout of the auxiliary verb "shall" rather than "should".

The articles are also an implicit statement of the *rights of all States* even though only expressed in terms of their obligations. For example, the obligation of any State to avoid or compensate for transboundary environmental impacts also involves a reciprocal right to protection against or compensation for harm caused to it by activities of or in other States.

7

Consequently, the adoption of such a set of mutual obligations and rights would be in both the common interests and self-interest of all States.

In this section of the report there is a brief introduction and summary of the main thrusts of each of the 22 articles. However, Annex 2 contains both the full texts in legal formulations and detailed "Comments" which include explanatory notes on the intent and application of each article as well as selected references to relevant precedents and cases.

The full texts in legal formulations in Annex 2 were approved by the members of the Experts Group, with the exception of Dr. Timoshenko as he was unfortunately unable to attend either meeting of the Experts Group but did provide comments and suggestions which were taken into account in the various drafts and development of the proposed legal principles. The texts in the "Comment" for each article were generally agreed to by the participants at the second meeting, but time did not permit either full review or endorsement in detail of them.

2. Key Terms Used

Regarding some of the key terminology used in the text, the Experts Group agreed to use the term "transboundary" rather than "transfrontier" as it seemed to have a wider application not only to natural resources and pollution crossing the frontiers of two or more States, but also to the boundary between areas under national jurisdiction and the global or regional commons. Moreover, the term "transboundary natural resources" also seemed to avoid some of the difficulties previously associated with the terms "shared" or "internationally shared" natural resources.

The Experts Group also agreed to use the term "transboundary environmental interferences" to embrace not only activities contributing to international pollution problems but also other environmental modifications with significant international effects (e.g. flooding, introduction of alien species, changes affecting regional or global climate, etc.).

More detailed and formal definitions for all of the key terms used in the 22 articles are provided at the beginning of Annex 2.

3. Summaries of the Legal Principles

The following *summaries* are based on the more detailed legal formulations of the 22 articles approved at the meeting of the WCED Experts Group on

Environmental Law which was held during 18–20 June 1986 at the Peace Palace in The Hague.

These summaries highlight *only* the main thrusts of the various articles. The summaries do not fully reflect all of the important qualifications and nuances in some of the key articles, and should therefore *not* be considered as substitutes for the original full texts in Annex 2.

Summary of Part I

General Principles, Rights and Obligations concerning Natural Resources and Environmental Interferences

1. Fundamental Human Right

Article 1 affirms that all human beings have the fundamental right to an environment adequate for their health and well-being.

2. Inter-Generational Equity

Article 2 stipulates that States shall conserve and use the environment and natural resources for the benefit of present and future generations.

3. Conservation* and Sustainable Use

Article 3 specifies that States shall maintain ecosystems and ecological processes essential for the functioning of the biosphere, to preserve biological diversity, and to observe the principle of optimum sustainable yield in the use of living natural resources and ecosystems.

---

*Throughout all of these articles "conservation" means the management of human use of a natural resource or the environment in such a manner that it may yield the greatest sustainable benefit to present generations while maintaining its potential to meet the needs and aspirations of future generations. It embraces preservation, maintenance, sustainable utilization, restoration, and enhancement of a natural resource or the environment.

4. Environmental Standards and Monitoring

Article 4 requires States to establish adequate environmental protection standards and to monitor changes in and publish relevant data on environmental quality and resource use.

5. Prior Environmental Assessments

Under Article 5, States must make or require environmental assessments of proposed activities which may significantly affect the environment or use of a natural resources.

6. Prior Notification, Access and Due Process

Under Article 6, States are obliged to inform in a timely manner all persons likely to be significantly affected by a planned activity and to grant them equal access and due process in administrative and judicial proceedings.

7. Sustainable Development and Assistance

Article 7 enjoins States to ensure that conservation is treated as an integral part of the planning and implementation of development activities and to provide assistance to other States, especially to developing countries, in support of environmental protection and sustainable development.

8. General Obligation to Co-operate

Article 8 affirms that States shall co-operate in good faith with other States in implementing the preceding rights and obligations.

Summary of Part II

Principles, Rights and Obligations Specifically concerning Transboundary Natural Resources and Environmental Interferences

9. Reasonable and Equitable Use

Article 9 enjoins States to use transboundary natural resources in a reasonable and equitable manner.

10. Prevention and Abatement

Article 10 requires States to prevent or abate any transboundary environmental interference which could cause or causes significant harm (but subject to certain exceptions provided for in Articles 11 and 12).

11. Strict Liability

Under Article 11, States may carry out or permit certain dangerous but beneficial activities provided they take all reasonable precautionary measures to limit the risk and ensure that compensation is provided should substantial transboundary harm occur. States shall also ensure that compensation is provided for substantial transboundary harm resulting from activities which were not known to be harmful at the time that they were undertaken.

12. Prior Agreements When Prevention Costs Greatly Exceed Harm

Article 12 provides that States which plan to carry out or permit activities causing transboundary harm which is substantial but far less than the cost of prevention shall enter into negotiations with the affected State on the equitable conditions under which the activity could be carried out. (If no agreement can be reached, Article 22 will apply).

13. Non-Discrimination

Article 13 requires States as a minimum to apply at least the same standards for environmental conduct and impacts regarding transboundary natural resources and environmental interferences as are applied domestically (i.e. do not do to others what you would not do to your own citizens).

14. General Obligation to Co-operate on Transboundary Environmental Problems

Article 14 affirms that States shall co-operate in good faith with other States to achieve optimal use of transboundary natural resources and effective prevention or abatement of transboundary environmental interferences.

15. Exchange of Information

Under Article 15, States of origin are obliged to provide timely and relevant information to the other concerned States regarding transboundary natural resources or environmental interferences.

16. Prior Assessment and Notification

Under Article 16, States must provide prior and timely notification and relevant information to the other concerned States, and make an environment assessment of planned activities which may have significant transboundary effects.

17. Prior Consultations

Article 17 stipulates that States of origin shall consult at an early stage and in good faith with other concerned States regarding existing or potential transboundary interferences with their use of a natural resource or the environment.

18. Co-operative Arrangements for Environmental Assessment and Protection

Article 18 specifies that States shall co-operate with the concerned States in monitoring, scientific research and standard setting regarding transboundary natural resources and environmental interferences.

19. Emergency Situations

Under Article 19, States are obliged to develop contingency plans regarding emergency situations likely to cause transboundary environmental interferences. States of origin must promptly warn, provide relevant information to and co-operate with concerned States when such emergencies occur.

20. Equal Access and Treatment

Under Article 20, States shall grant all persons who are and may be affected by transboundary interferences, with their use of a natural resource or the environment with equal access, due process and equal treatment in administrative and judicial proceedings.

Summary of Part III

21. State Responsibility

Article 21 obliges States to cease activities which breach an international obligation regarding the environment and to provide compensation for the harm caused.

Summary of Part IV

22. Peaceful Settlement of Disputes

Article 22 affirms that States shall settle environmental disputes by peaceful means. It further requires that if mutual agreement is not reached within 18 months on a solution or on other dispute settlement arrangements, the dispute shall be submitted to conciliation and, if unresolved, thereafter to arbitration or judicial settlement at the request of any of the concerned States.

PROPOSALS FOR STRENGTHENING THE LEGAL AND INSTITUTIONAL FRAMEWORK

As noted earlier, the Experts Group met only twice for a total of five working days of discussion, with the main focus on developing and refining the concepts and legal formulations for the 22 articles set out in Annex 2.

In spite of the severe time constraints for discussion, the participants at the second meeting of the Experts Group also reached general agreement on a series of recommendations to the Commission for strengthening the legal and institutional framework for accelerating the development and application of international law in support of environmental protection and sustainable development within and among all States.

The following recommendations reflect the main thrust of the principal concerns and views of the participants at the second meeting of the Experts Group, as time did not permit their full development or approval in detail. Further variations of some of the recommendations could be made. For example, the proposals for setting up a special United Nations Commission and/or appointing an international "ombudsman" are in the following text both linked to the preceding recommendation for a new universal convention or covenant, but either proposal could also be considered on its own merits and launched without such a link by proceeding with elections by the UN General Assembly.

The recommendations for consideration by the World Commission are briefly set out below.

1. Establish a New Legal Basis for Environmental Protection and Sustainable Development

It is recommended that a new and legally-binding universal Convention be prepared under United Nations auspices.

(a) The Convention should consolidate existing and establish new legal principles, and set out the associated rights and responsibilities of States individually and collectively for securing environmental protection and sustainable development to the year 2000 and beyond.

(b) The Convention should also include effective measures for protecting those rights and for fulfilling those responsibilities.

(c) The UN General Assembly should establish a special negotiating group to prepare a text for signature by States during or preferably before 1992, the 20th anniversary of the United Nations Conference on the Human Environment.

2. Set Up a Special UN Commission

It is recommended that a special UN Commission for Environmental Protection and Sustainable Development be established under the above Convention.

(a) The special Commission should have a limited but representative membership consisting of competent individuals serving in a personal capacity who are elected preferably by secret ballot by States Parties to the Convention.

(b) The special Commission should receive and review regular reports from States and from relevant organizations of the UN system and other concerned international organizations and non-governmental organizations on actions they have taken to implement the Convention.

(c) Other main functions of the special Commission would include: (a) to issue periodic public reports on progress in implementing the Convention and other relevant international agreements; (b) to assess and report on alleged violations; (c) to receive and review recommendations and proposals for improved implementation or extension of the Convention and other relevant international agreements.

3. Appoint an International "Ombudsman"

It is recommended that a UN High Commissioner for Environmental Protection and Sustainable Development (with some functions similar to an "ombudsman" and "trustee" for environment) be elected preferably by secret ballot by the States Parties to the above Convention.

(a) The High Commissioner would receive and assess communications from private organizations and individuals concerning compliance with or violations of the above Convention or related international agreements. The High Commissioner could submit any such cases for consideration to the special UN Commission or other appropriate international organizations (e.g. UNEP).

(b) The High Commissioner would have special responsibilities regarding the protection and use of areas beyond national jurisdiction, and for representing and protecting the interests of future generations.

(c) The High Commissioner would also prepare and publish, in co-operation with key scientific and UN bodies such as UNEP, special reports with recommendations regarding the state of the world's natural and cultural heritage, and particularly on environmentally-based situations and conditions threatening critical ecological systems and processes which could increase economic, social and political instability within and among States.

4. Strengthen the Existing Global and Regional Legal Framework

It is recommended that States:

(a) accede to or ratify global and regional conventions dealing with environment and development;

(b) adhere more rigorously to the provisions, spirit and objectives of existing conventions relevant to environment and development;

(c) review and revise existing conventions relevant to environment and development in order to bring them in line with the latest available technical and scientific information;

(d) enter into new global and regional conventions or arrangements aimed at promoting co-operation and co-ordination in the field of environment and development (including, for example, new conventions on biological diversity and on high risk technologies);

(e) include a legal expert with special competence and experience on environmental and resources management issues on all delegations to relevant treaty negotiations and conferences;

(f) adopt at the national level adequate legal guidelines based on the "General Principles concerning Natural Resources and Environmental Interferences", with the advice and assistance of relevant international organizations such as UNEP.

5. Increase the Capacity to Avoid and Settle Disputes

It is recommended that intergovernmental and non-governmental organizations which maintain panels or rosters of those with experience and competence in various forms of dispute settlement include and indicate on their rosters those with special experience and competence on legal and substantive aspects of environmental protection and natural resources management.

It is recommended that "clearing house" services be established on global, regional and national levels to assist in the avoidance or settlement of environment and resources disputes. The service:

(a) should, where possible, use existing institutions;

(b) should be available to States and other natural or juridical persons;

(c) should include a range of dispute avoidance or settlement mechanisms including fact finding, good offices, mediation, conciliation, arbitration and judicial settlement;

(d) should develop a roster of available experts for each of the above categories;

(e) should be well publicized.

It is recommended that States, when unable to resolve any dispute concerning a transboundary natural resource or environmental interference within a reasonable time, agree to submit any such case for binding arbitration or judicial settlement to, for example, the Permanent Court of Arbitration or the International Court of Justice.

(a) Regarding the Permanent Court of Arbitration, those States with the right to select four members of the Court should give special consideration to ensuring that at least one of the four members has special legal experience and competence on questions of environmental protection and natural resources management.

(b) Regarding the International Court of Justice, the Court (under Article 26 of the Statute of the Court) can form special chambers for dealing with particular cases or categories of cases, including environmental protection or resources management cases. The Court has recently emphasized its readiness to deal with such cases fully and promptly, and States should consider making more use of this capacity for avoiding prolonged disputes.

6. Launch New Initiative of Non-Governmental Organizations on Implementing International Agreements

It is recommended that non-governmental organizations establish special committees or groups at global and regional levels: (a) to encourage States to accept and implement international agreements related to environmental protection and sustainable development, especially those which have not entered into force because they lack the minimum number or acceptance needed; (b) to monitor compliance with such agreements; and (c) to publish periodic reports on acceptances still needed, and on any violations of the agreements.

7. Expand Participation and Standing of Non-Governmental Organizations

It is recommended that international intergovernmental organizations that engage in activities relating to environmental protection and development should establish procedures for official consultative status for and consultations with capable and qualified non-governmental organizations.

It is also recommended that all States should accord capable and qualified non-governmental organizations concerned with environmental protection and sustainable development the right to consult with all relevant agencies and political sub-divisions of the State with respect to protecting and conserving the environment. States should provide the above groups with *locus standi* to present evidence that the environment is not being adequately protected. Proceedings in such cases should be open and decisions made public.

8. Extend Environmental Responsibilities of Private Enterprises

It is recommended that multinational enterprises accept and implement on a world-wide basis the principles already adopted within OECD as a clarification of the OECD Guiding Principles for Multinational Enterprises of which the main thrusts read:

> "Enterprises, whether they are domestic or multinational, should within the framework of laws, regulations and administrative practices in each of the countries in which they operate, take due account of the need to protect the environment and to avoid creating environmentally-related health problems."

> "Enterprises should in particular:

> (a) assess and take into account in decision making the foreseeable consequences of their activities which could significantly affect the environment;

> (b) co-operate with competent authorities, inter alia, by providing adequate and timely information regarding the potential impacts on the environment and on environmentally related health aspects of all their activities and by providing the relevant expertise available in the enterprise as a whole;

> (c) take appropriate measures in their operations to minimize the risk of accidents and damage to the environment, and to co-operate in mitigating adverse environmental effects, in particular:

> —by selecting and adopting appropriate technologies and practices compatible with those objectives;

> —by implementing education and training programmes for their employees;

> —by preparing contingency plans; and

> —by enabling their competent entities to be adequately equipped, especially by providing them with adequate knowledge and assistance."[1]

It is recommended that private banks and other financial institutions that provide funds for development projects should require an assessment of the environmental effects and sustainability as part of the evaluation process for projects for which loans are requested.

---

[1] See *International Legal Materials*, Vol. 25, No. 2 (1986), p. 494.

9. Apply Criminal Liability for Environmental Damage

It is recommended that effective criminal liability be established and applied by States for actions of their nationals which have a detrimental effect upon the environment, in particular on ecosystems and species of international significance, and including those actions in areas beyond the limits of national jurisdiction.

10. Assess Risks of New Technologies

It is recommended that States establish:

(a) a special international capacity or system for monitoring and assessing risks regarding new technologies, including chemicals and biotechnology, which may have significant effects on human health, the environment or natural resources;

(b) guidelines and standards to reduce those risks in the conduct of experiments, or in the production, transport, and use of new technologies and products;

(c) international networks for the collection and dissemination of information on such new technologies and products.

11. Adopt Basic Safety and Notification Measures for Nuclear Power Installations

It is recommended that States adopt as a matter of priority basic international safety standards for the design, construction and operation of nuclear power installations as well as measures for regular safety inspections; and (b) make it mandatory for all public authorities to make all relevant information public without delay whenever they have been notified of any harmful or potentially harmful release of pollutants, especially radioactive releases.

12. Increase Environmental Education and Expertise

It is recommended that States increase the emphasis on and support for environmental information and education programmes as a major and integral part of all primary, secondary school and university curricula as well as in professional and other in-service training courses, with particular attention to the relationship between environmental protection and sustainable development.

It is recommended that States give particular encouragement and support to specialized education programmes for training experts on the scientific, technical, economic and legal aspects of environmental protection and sustainable development.

13. Avoid Severe Environmental Damage from Armed Conflicts

It is recommended that all parties involved in an international or even purely national armed conflict abstain from methods or means of warfare which are intended, or may be expected, to cause widespread, long-lasting or severe damages to the environment (e.g. nuclear, biological or chemical weapons; weather or other major environmental modification techniques).

ANNEX 1

LIST OF BACKGROUND AND DISCUSSION PAPERS

First Experts Group Meeting (June 1985)

Lammers, J. G., *Concepts and Principles of International Law concerning the Use of Shared Natural Resources and Transfrontier Environmental Interferences* (Draft Outline for Discussion).
Summary Date Sheets on Principles Proposed for Discussion (EGEL/685/2).
WCED Draft Programme and Workplan on International Co-operation (EGEL/685/2).
Rules of International Law Applicable to Transfrontier Pollution (EGEL/685/4).
IUCN Environmental Law Centre, *Status of Multilateral Conventions Related to Environment* (EGEL/685/5).

Interim Reports (July 1985 to May 1986)

Summary Report of the First Meeting (WCED/85/CRD.2/Annex 7).
Reports by the Rapporteur on Principles of and for International Environmental Law (three consecutive working drafts).

Legal Principles for Environmental Protection and Sustainable Development (Discussion Paper for the
Fourth Meeting of the Commission) (WCED/85/24A).
Stein, R. E., and Grenville-Wood, G., *The Settlement of Environmental Disputes: A Forward Look*
(Discussion Paper for the Fourth Meeting of the Commission) (WCED/85/24B).

Second Experts Group Meeting (June 1986)

Report by the Rapporteur on Principles of and for International Environmental Law (EGEL/686/2).
Strengthening International Legal Institutions and Processes (EGEL/686/3), including the *Fortieth
Anniversary Statement by the President of the International Court of Justice* (Annex 1), a *Proposal to
Strengthen the Permanent Court of Arbitration* (Annex 2), and a *Proposal for a World Tribunal for
Environmental Protection* (Annex 3).
Multilateral Conventions Related to Environment (EGEL/686/4).
IUCN Commission on Environmental Policy, Law and Administration, *Proposals for Interna-
tional Environmental Law Developments Towards the Year 2000*.
IUCN, *World Charter for Nature: Commentary, Part II*.
Quebec Minister of Environment, *Proposal for an International Code of Ethics for the Environment*.

ANNEX 2

FINAL REPORT OF THE EXPERTS GROUP ON ENVIRONMENTAL LAW ON LEGAL PRINCIPLES FOR ENVIRONMENTAL PROTECTION AND SUSTAINABLE DEVELOPMENT

(See for this Final Report *infra* pp. 35–143.)

ELEMENTS FOR A DRAFT CONVENTION ON ENVIRONMENTAL PROTECTION AND SUSTAINABLE DEVELOPMENT

adopted by the

EXPERTS GROUP ON ENVIRONMENTAL LAW

June 1986

GENERAL PRINCIPLES CONCERNING NATURAL RESOURCES AND ENVIRONMENTAL INTERFERENCES

Article 1
Fundamental human right

All human beings have the fundamental right to an environment adequate for their health and well-being.

Article 2
Conservation for present and future generations

States shall ensure that the environment and natural resources are conserved and used for the benefit of present and future generations.

Article 3
Ecosystems, related ecological processes, biological diversity, and sustainability

States shall:

(a) maintain ecosystems and related ecological processes essential for the functioning of the biosphere in all its diversity, in particular those important for food production, health and other aspects of human survival and sustainable development;

(b) maintain maximum biological diversity by ensuring the survival and promoting the conservation in their natural habitat of all species of fauna and flora, in particular those which are rare, endemic or endangered;

(c) observe, in the exploitation of living natural resources and ecosystems, the principle of optimum sustainable yield.

Article 4
Environmental standards and monitoring

States shall:

(a) establish specific environmental standards, in particular environmental quality standards, emission standards, technological standards and product standards, aimed at preventing or abating interferences with natural resources or the environment;

(b) establish systems for the collection and dissemination of data and regular observation of natural resources and the environment in order to permit adequate planning of the use of natural resources and the environment, to permit early detection of interferences with natural resources or the environment and ensure timely intervention, and to facilitate the evaluation of conservation policies and methods.

Article 5
Assessment of planned activities

States planning to carry out or permit activities which may significantly affect a natural resource or the environment shall make or require an assessment of their effects before carrying out or permitting the planned activities.

Article 6
Timely information, access and due process

States shall inform all persons in a timely manner of activities which may significantly affect their use of a natural resource or their environment and shall grant the concerned persons access to and due process in administrative and judicial proceedings.

Article 7
Planning and implementation of development activities

1. States shall ensure that the conservation of natural resources and the environment is treated as an integral part of the planning and implementation of development activities. Particular attention shall be

paid to environmental problems arising in developing countries and to the need to incorporate environmental considerations in all development assistance programmes.

2. States shall make available to other States, and especially to developing countries, upon their request and under agreed terms scientific and technical information and expertise, results of research programmes, training opportunities and specialized equipment and facilities which are needed by such other States to promote rational use of natural resources, and the environment or to prevent or abate interference with natural resources or the environment, in particular in cases of environmental emergencies.

Article 8
General obligation to co-operate

States shall co-operate in good faith with other States or through competent international organizations in the implementation of the provisions of the preceding articles.

PRINCIPLES SPECIFICALLY CONCERNING TRANSBOUNDARY NATURAL RESOURCES AND ENVIRONMENTAL INTERFERENCES

Article 9
Reasonable and equitable use of transboundary natural resources

States shall use transboundary natural resources in a reasonable and equitable manner.

Article 10
Prevention and abatement of a transboundary environmental interference

States shall, without prejudice to the principles laid down in Articles 11 and 12, prevent or abate any transboundary environmental interference or a significant risk thereof which causes substantial harm—i.e. harm which is not minor or insignificant.

Article 11
Liability for transboundary environmental interferences resulting from lawful activities

1. If one or more activities create a significant risk of substantial harm as a result of a transboundary environmental interference, and if the overall technical and socio-economic cost or loss of benefits involved in preventing or reducing such risk far exceeds in the long run the advantage which such prevention or reduction would entail, the State which carried out or permitted the activities shall ensure that compensation is provided should substantial harm occur in an area under national jurisdiction of another State or in an area beyond the limits of national jurisdiction.

2. A State shall ensure that compensation is provided for substantial harm caused by transboundary environmental interferences resulting from activities carried out or permitted by that State notwithstanding that the activities were not initially known to cause such interferences.

Article 12
Transboundary environmental interferences involving substantial harm far less than cost of prevention

1. If a State is planning to carry out or permit an activity which will entail a transboundary environmental interference causing harm which is substantial but far less than the overall technical and socio-economic cost or loss of benefits involved in preventing or reducing such interference, such State shall enter into negotiations with the affected State on the equitable conditions, both technical and financial, under which the activity could be carried out.

2. In the event of a failure to reach a solution on the basis of equitable principles within a period of 18 months after the beginning of the negotiations or within any other period of time agreed upon by the States concerned, the dispute shall at the request of any of the States concerned, and under the conditions set forth in Paragraphs 3

and 4 of Article 22, be submitted to conciliation or thereafter to arbitration or judicial settlement in order to reach a solution on the basis of equitable principles.

Article 13
Non-discrimination between domestic and transboundary environmental interferences

Without prejudice to the principles laid down in Articles 10, 11 and 12 when calling for a more stringent approach, States shall, when considering under their domestic policy or law the permissibility of an environmental interference or a significant risk thereof, take into account the detrimental effects which are or may be caused by the environmental interference without discrimination as to whether the effects would occur inside or outside the area under their national jurisdiction.

Article 14
General obligation to co-operate on transboundary environmental problems

1. States shall co-operate in good faith with the other States concerned in maintaining or attaining for each of them a reasonable and equitable use of a transboundary natural resource or in preventing or abating a transboundary environmental interference or significant risk thereof.
2. The co-operation shall, as much as possible, be aimed at arriving at an optimal use of the transboundary natural resource or at maximizing the effectiveness of measures to prevent or abate a transboundary environmental interference.

Article 15
Exchange of information

States shall provide the other States concerned upon their request and in a timely manner with all relevant and reasonably available data concerning a transboundary natural resource, including the uses made of such a resource and transboundary interferences with them, or concerning a transboundary environmental interference.

Article 16
Prior notice of planned activities, environmental impact assessments

1. States planning to carry out or permit activities which may entail a transboundary interference or a significant risk thereof with the reasonable and equitable use of a transboundary natural resource or which may entail a transboundary environmental interference or a significant risk thereof causing substantial harm in an area under national jurisdiction of another State or in an area beyond the limits of national jurisdiction shall give timely notice to the States concerned. In particular, they shall on their own initiative or upon request of the other States concerned provide such relevant information as will permit those other States to make an assessment of the probable effects of the planned activities.

2. When a State has reasonable grounds for believing that planned activities may have the effects referred to in Paragraph 1, it shall make an assessment of those effects before carrying out or permitting the planned activities.

Article 17
Consultations

Consultations shall be held in good faith, upon request, at an early stage between, on the one hand, States whose reasonable and equitable use of a transboundary natural resource is or may be affected by a transboundary interference or whose environmental interests are or may be affected by a transboundary environmental interference and, on the other hand, States in whose area under national jurisdiction or under whose jurisdiction such a transboundary interference originates or may originate in connection with activities carried on or contemplated therein or thereunder.

Article 18
Co-operative arrangements for environmental assessment and protection

In order to maintain or attain a reasonable and equitable use of a transboundary natural resource or to prevent or abate transboundary environmental interferences or significant risks thereof the States concerned shall, inter alia:

(a) establish co-ordinated or unified systems for the collection and dissemination of data relating to the transboundary natural resource or for regular observation of transboundary environmental interferences;

(b) co-ordinate and, where appropriate, jointly undertake scientific or technical studies to that effect;

(c) establish by common agreement specific environmental standards, in particular environmental quality standards and emission standards;

(d) jointly establish or resort to an institutional mechanism or other appropriate arrangement.

Article 19
Emergency situations

1. In the case of an emergency situation or other change of circumstances suddenly giving rise to a transboundary interference or a significant risk thereof with the reasonable and equitable use of a transboundary natural resource or to a transboundary environmental interference or a significant risk thereof, causing substantial harm in an area under national jurisdiction of another State or in an area beyond the limits of national jurisdiction, the State in whose area under national jurisdiction or under whose jurisdiction the interference originates shall promptly warn the other States concerned, provide them with such pertinent information as will enable them to minimize the transboundary environmental interference, inform them of steps taken to abate the cause of the transboundary environmental interference, and co-operate with those States in order to prevent or minimize the harmful effects of such an emergency situation or other change of circumstances.

2. States shall develop contingency plans in order to prevent or minimize the harmful effects of an emergency situation or other change of circumstances referred to in Paragraph 1.

Article 20
Non-intergovernmental proceedings

States shall provide remedies for persons who have been or may be detrimentally affected by a transboundary interference with their use of a transboundary natural resource or by a transboundary environmental interference. In particular, States of origin shall grant those persons equal access as well as due process and equal treatment in the same administrative and judicial proceedings as are available to persons within their own jurisdiction who have been or may be similarly affected.

STATE RESPONSIBILITY

Article 21

1. A State is responsible under international law for a breach of an international obligation relating to the use of a natural resource or the prevention or abatement of an environmental interference.

2. In particular, it shall:

(a) cease the internationally wrongful act;

(b) as far as possible, re-establish the situation which would have existed if the internationally wrongful act had not taken place;

(c) provide compensation for the harm which results from the internationally wrongful act;

(d) where appropriate, give satisfaction for the internationally wrongful act.

PEACEFUL SETTLEMENT OF DISPUTES

Article 22

1. States, when they cannot avoid international disputes concerning the use of a natural resource or concerning an environmental interfer-

ence in accordance with the preceding articles, shall settle such disputes by peaceful means in such a manner that international peace and security, and justice, are not endangered.

2. States shall accordingly seek a settlement of such disputes by negotiation, good offices, enquiry, mediation, conciliation, arbitration, judicial settlement, resort to appropriate bodies or arrangements, whether global or regional, or by any other peaceful means of their own choice.

3. In the event of a failure to reach a solution by another non-binding peaceful means within a period of 18 months after the dispute has arisen or within any other period of time agreed upon by the States concerned, the dispute shall be submitted to conciliation at the request of any of the States concerned, unless it is agreed to proceed with an already agreed peaceful means or to submit the dispute to another binding or non-binding means of peaceful settlement.

4. In the event that the conciliation envisaged in Paragraph 3, or any other non-binding means of peaceful settlement resorted to in lieu thereof, does not lead to a solution of the dispute, the dispute shall be submitted to arbitration or judicial settlement at the request of any of the States concerned, unless it is agreed to submit the dispute to another means of peaceful settlement.

FINAL REPORT OF THE EXPERTS GROUP ON ENVIRONMENTAL LAW ON LEGAL PRINCIPLES FOR ENVIRONMENTAL PROTECTION AND SUSTAINABLE DEVELOPMENT

June 1986

CONTENTS

STATE RESPONSIBILITY

PEACEFUL SETTLEMENT OF DISPUTES

ANNEX: LIST OF INTERNATIONAL AGREEMENTS AND OTHER INSTRUMENTS

LEGAL PRINCIPLES FOR ENVIRONMENTAL PROTECTION AND SUSTAINABLE DEVELOPMENT

USE OF TERMS

For the purposes of the present text:

(a) "use of a natural resource" means any human conduct, which, directly or indirectly, takes advantage of the benefits of a natural resource in the form of preservation, exploitation, consumption or otherwise of the natural resource, in so far as it does not result in an environmental interference as defined in Paragraph (f);

(b) "interference with the use of a natural resource" means any impairment, directly or indirectly, by man of the use of a natural resource in so far as it does not constitute an environmental interference as defined in Paragraph (f);

(c) "transboundary natural resource" means a natural resource which physically crosses the boundary between an area under the national jurisdiction of a State and an area under the national jurisdiction of another State or an area beyond the limits of national jurisdiction to the extent that its use in an area under the national jurisdiction of one State may affect its use in an area under the national jurisdiction of another State or in an area beyond the limits of national jurisdiction or vice versa;

(d) "transboundary interference with the use of a transboundary natural resource" means an interference with the use of a natural resource of which the physical origin is wholly or in part located outside the area under national jurisdiction of a State or outside the area beyond the limits of national jurisdiction in which the use takes place;

(e) "international natural resource" means a natural resource physi-

37

cally within an area beyond the limits of national jurisdiction to the extent that the origin and effects of any impairment of the use of the natural resource remain within the area beyond the limits of national jurisdiction;

(f) "environmental interference" means any impairment of human health, living resources, ecosystems, material property, amenities or other legitimate uses of a natural resource or the environment caused, directly or indirectly, by man through polluting substances, ionizing radiation, noise, explosions, vibration or other forms of energy, plants, animals, diseases, flooding, sand-drift or other similar means;

(g) "transboundary environmental interference" means an environmental interference of which the physical origin is wholly or in part located either outside the area under national jurisdiction of a State in which the effects caused by the interference occur, or outside the area beyond the limits of national jurisdiction in which the effects caused by the interference occur;

(h) "international environmental interference" means an environmental interference of which the physical origin and the effects are located within an area beyond the limits of national jurisdiction;

(i) "conservation" means the management of human use of a natural resource or the environment in such a manner that it may yield the greatest sustainable benefit to present generations while maintaining its potential to meet the needs and aspirations of future generations. It embraces preservation, maintenance, sustainable utilization, restoration and enhancement of a natural resource or the environment.

GENERAL PRINCIPLES CONCERNING NATURAL RESOURCES AND ENVIRONMENTAL INTERFERENCES

Article 1
Fundamental human right

All human beings have the fundamental right to an environment adequate for their health and well-being.

Comment

This article stipulates the fundamental right of every individual human being to an environment adequate for his health and well-being. The formulation of this fundamental right differs in various respects from that proclaimed in Principle 1 of the 1972 UN Declaration on the Human Environment which provides:

> "Man has the fundamental right to freedom, equality and adequate conditions of life, in an environment of a quality that permits a life of dignity and well-being . . . ."

The formulated fundamental right is to be preferred to the one contained in Principle 1 of the 1972 UN Declaration. Firstly, because its *direct* and *immediate* object is the maintenance and/or restoration of an adequate environment. The principle in the 1972 UN Declaration on the contrary has as its direct and immediate object "freedom, equality and adequate conditions of life", putting the requirement of an adequate environment merely in second place. Secondly, the formulated fundamental right refers to the more concrete notion of "health" as an interest to be protected and avoids an explicit reference to the concept of "a life of dignity", which may be deemed to be comprised in the notion of "well-being".

Although the environment to which the fundamental right formulated above relates clearly comprises the environment in which human beings live, it also is intended to comprise those parts of the earth and the surrounding sphere which hold important natural resources for man (e.g. marine waters) or which, when disturbed or degraded, may eventually detrimentally affect areas normally inhabited by man (e.g. rain forests or the ozone layer).

Of course, the requirement that the environment must be "adequate for [human] health and well-being" is extremely vague. In any case both physical and mental health and well-being are to be protected and promoted. The adjective "adequate" makes clear that there are limits to the protection of the environment for the purpose of promoting the health and well-being of human beings. Indeed, those limits may to some extent even be dictated by the need to promote the health or well-being of human beings (e.g. by food production or housing). Apart from that, the determination of the adequacy of the environment for the health and well-being of human beings will depend to a considerable extent on many regional or local factors, such as the nature of the environment concerned, the kind of use made of it, the means at the disposal of the public authorities and the population, and the expectations of the human beings themselves.

The fundamental human right to an adequate environment implies at least the existence of an international obligation on the part of States vis-à-vis other States, if not also vis-à-vis individual human beings, to adequately protect the environment for the benefit of individual human beings (substantive human right) and/or to grant to such individual human beings the procedural legal means necessary to protect their interests in an adequate environment (procedural human right) against infringements by the State or by other entities or persons (e.g. private companies or individuals).

By postulating in Article 1 the fundamental human right to an adequate environment, it is made clear that the obligations of States formulated in the subsequent articles are not merely intended to protect the interests of States *inter se* in maintaining or restoring an adequate environment, but also those of individual human beings irrespective of their nationality. Moreover, Article 2 makes clear that these obligations do not merely exist in the interest of *present* human beings, but also for the benefit of *future* generations.

Article 1 only purports to establish a fundamental right of human beings to an adequate environment vis-à-vis other human beings or entities created by man such as States. In other words the emphasis laid in Article 1 on the protection of the interests of human beings may not be deemed to imply a choice for an anthropocentric approach in environmental questions.

It cannot be said that the fundamental human right to an adequate environment already constitutes a well-established right under present international law. As a matter of fact there are as yet no treaties which provide for a specific human right to an adequate environment. Efforts made within the framework of the Council of Europe during the 1970s to adopt such a human right in an additional protocol to the 1950 European Convention for the Protection of Human Rights and Fundamental Freedoms or through an amendment of the 1961 European Social Charter unfortunately failed to obtain the required support. It is true that the 1974 Nordic Environmental Protection Convention grants inhabitants of a country who are (possibly) detrimentally affected by a (planned) environmentally harmful activity in another country, a right of equal access to and of equal treatment by the administrative or judicial authorities of the latter country. However, this convention does not provide for an *independent* (substantive and/or procedural) right to an adequate environment for the inhabitants of the country of origin of the environmentally harmful activity and consequently neither for the inhabitants of countries (possibly) affected by such an activity. The argument of the absence of an independent right to an adequate environment applies, of course, likewise to all those OECD or other recommendations which recommend the granting of a right of equal access or treatment to individuals (possibly) affected by a transboundary environmental interference.

Certain treaties provide for human rights which may imply a corollary duty not to impair the environment beyond a certain degree. Reference may be made here to the inherent right to life of every human being stated in Article 6(1) of the 1966 UN Covenant on Civil and Political Rights. However, it should be kept in mind that this right can only be invoked when the environmental degradation has reached such an extent that life itself is endangered, so that it must be deemed to be of little use to safeguard a certain *quality* of life. Another limitation is to be found in the last sentence of Article 6(1) which provides that "No one shall be *arbitrarily* deprived of his life." (emphasis added).

Certain provisions in the 1966 UN Covenant on Economic, Social and Cultural Rights are more promising. The States parties to this covenant recognize in Article 11(1) ". . . the right of everyone to an *adequate standard of living* . . . and to the *continuous improvement of living conditions*" (emphasis added) and in Article 12(1) ". . . the right of everyone to the enjoyment of the *highest attainable standard of physical and mental health*", the full realization of which is to be achieved, inter alia, by "the improvement of all aspects of *environmental* . . . *hygiene*" (emphasis added). It is clear that the realization of the right to an adequate standard of living and to the highest attainable standard of physical and mental health may well require the taking of measures to prevent or abate impairment of the environment. However, it should also be borne in mind that, according to the 1966 UN Covenant on Economic, Social and Cultural Rights (see Article 2(1)), the realization of these rights need only be progressively achieved by States which are a party to the covenant "by all appropriate means" and "to the maximum of [their] available resources".

En dehors treaties, some indirect support for a right of human beings to an adequate environment also may be found in everyone's right to life (Article 3) or everyone's right to a standard of living adequate for the health and well-being of himself and of his family (Article 25) which are proclaimed in UNGA Resolution No. 217 of 10 December 1948 adopting the Universal Declaration of Human Rights. Noteworthy, however, also is Article 29(2) which provides that the rights proclaimed in the Universal Declaration may be limited by law "for the purpose of . . . meeting the just requirements of . . . the general welfare in a democratic society". Like the 1966 UN Covenant on Economic, Social and Cultural Rights, the Universal Declaration sets only certain standards of achievement (see the Preamble), but, unlike the 1966 UN Covenant, does not constitute a legally binding instrument for States.

Reference to a specific international human right to an adequate environment is, in fact, only to be found in the above-quoted Principle 1 of the 1972 UN Declaration on the Human Environment. Apart from the fact that the States which adopted the 1972 UN Declaration probably regarded the principle as not legally binding but stating merely a goal to be achieved, there also remains the problem of the clear incompatibility of the proclaimed fundamental human right with the statement in Principle 21 of the 1972 UN Declaration that: "States have, in accordance with the Charter of the United Nations and the principles of international law, the sovereign right to exploit their own resources pursuant to their own environmental policies . . .". This sovereign right is, in Principle 21, only restricted in case damage is caused to the environment of other States or of areas beyond the limits of national jurisdiction.

The source of many human rights which have eventually found recognition on the international plane is to be found in municipal law. Hence, support for an emerging specific fundamental human right to an adequate environment may possibly be found in national constitutional or other legislation. While there are a fair number of constitutional or other legal provisions which impose a basic duty on the State to protect (certain parts of) the environment, there are only very few provisions which provide for a specific right of individual human beings to an adequate environment (see, e.g. Article 45(1) of the 1978 Constitution of Spain; Article 123 of the 1979 Constitution of Peru; and perhaps Article 71 of the 1976 Polish Constitution) or provide that the State must protect the environment for the benefit of individual human beings. Hence, it is as yet not possible to maintain that there already exists a general principle of (national) law recognized by civilized nations in the sense of article 38(1)(c) of the Statute of the International Court of Justice which embodies a fundamental human right to an adequate environment.

The fundamental human right laid down in Article 1 therefore remains an ideal which must still be realized.

Article 2
Conservation for present and future generations

States shall ensure that the environment and natural resources are conserved and used for the benefit of present and future generations.

Comment

The present article stipulates that the environment and natural resources are to serve the needs of both present *and future* generations. It purports to give effect to the statement in the Preamble of the 1972 UN Declaration on the Human Environment that: "To defend and improve the human environment for present *and future* generations has become an imperative goal for mankind . . ." (emphasis added). It obliges States to manage the environment and natural resources for the benefit of present generations in such a way that they are held in trust for future generations.

This implies, in the first place, a basic obligation for States to conserve options for future generations by maintaining to the maximum extent possible the diversity of the natural resource base. It requires a management of natural resources or the environment in such a manner that they may yield the greatest sustainable benefit to present generations while maintaining their potential to meet the needs and aspirations of future generations. Conservation of the diversity of the natural resource base for the benefit of future generations is warranted as the possibilities to develop substitute products or to improve production and/or extraction technologies are not unlimited. Or else because future generations may otherwise only be able to obtain the same benefits at considerably higher costs.

The second basic obligation for States following from the duty to hold the natural heritage of mankind in trust for future generations, concerns the prevention or abatement of pollution or other forms of degradation of natural resources or the environment, which would reduce the range of uses to which the natural resources or environment could be put or which would confront future generations with enormous financial burdens to clean up the environment.

Support for the duty of States to ensure that the natural heritage of mankind is used and conserved for the benefit of both present and future generations is to be found in many international instruments.

Thus, Principle 1 of the 1972 UN Declaration on the Human Environment provides that: "Man . . . bears a solemn responsibility to protect and improve the environment for present and future generations". Principle 2 of the 1972 UN Declaration lays down that: "The natural resources of the earth including the air, water, land, flora and fauna and especially representative samples of natural ecosystems must be safeguarded for the benefit of present and future generations through careful planning or management, as appropriate." Principle 5 provides that: "The non-renewable resources of the earth must be employed in such a way as to guard against the danger of their future exhaustion . . .", while Principle 6 states that: "The discharge of toxic substances or of other substances and the release of heat, in such quantities or concentrations as to exceed the capacity of the environment to render them harmless, must be halted in order to ensure that serious or irreversible damage is not inflicted on ecosystems . . .".

Numerous references to the need to conserve the natural heritage of mankind for the benefit of present and future generations also are to be found (usually in the preamble) in many international agreements concluded after the adoption of the 1972 UN Declaration on the Human Environment, e.g. in:

1972 Paris Convention concerning the Protection of World Cultural and Natural Heritage;
1973 Washington Convention on International Trade in Endangered Species of Wild Fauna and Flora;
1976 Barcelona Convention for the Mediterranean Sea;
1976 Apia Convention on the Conservation of Nature in the South Pacific;
1977 Geneva Convention on the Prohibition of Military or Any Other Hostile Use of Environmental Modification Techniques;
1978 Kuwait Regional Convention;
1979 Berne Convention on the Conservation of European Wildlife and Natural Habitats;
1979 Bonn Convention on the Conservation of Migratory Species of Wild Animals;
1983 Cartagena de Indias Convention for the Wider Caribbean Region; and
1985 ASEAN Agreement on the Conservation of Nature and Natural Resources.

Reference must also be made to Article 30 of the Charter of Economic Rights and Duties of States proclaimed in UNGA Resolution No. 3281; to UNGA Resolution No. 36/7 of 27 October 1981 on the Historical Responsibility of States for the Presevation of Nature for Present and Future Generations; and to UNGA Resolution No. 37/7 of 28 October 1982 on the World Charter for Nature.

Although in the preceding observations special emphasis has been laid on the obligation to conserve natural resources and the environment for the benefit of *future* generations, one should not forget that such an obligation also exists for the benefit of *present* generations. The basic obligation for the benefit of both present and future generations is further elaborated in the following articles.

To the extent that this basic obligation concerns international or transboundary natural resources or environmental interferences, it already may in many respects be deemed to find substantial support in existing general international law.

In this connection it may finally be observed that the conservation or use of the environment and natural resources for the benefit of present and future generations also implies certain restraints for the parties to an international or non-international armed conflict in that they shall abstain from methods or means of warfare which are intended, or may be expected, to cause widespread, long-lasting or severe damage to the environment. Support for this idea may, inter alia, be found in the 1977 Geneva Convention on the Prohibition of Military or Any Other Hostile Use of Environmental Modification Techniques.

Article 3
Ecosystems, related ecological processes, biological diversity, and sustainability

States shall:

(a) maintain ecosystems and related ecological processes essential for the functioning of the biosphere in all its diversity, in particular those important for food production, health and other aspects of human survival and sustainable development;

(b) maintain maximum biological diversity by ensuring the survival and promoting the conservation in their natural habitat of all species of fauna and flora, in particular those which are rare, endemic or endangered;

(c) observe, in the exploitation of living natural resources and ecosystems, the principle of optimum sustainable yield.

Comment

Paragraph (a) of the present article obliges States to maintain ecosystems— i.e. systems of plants, animals and micro-organisms together with the non-living components of their environment—and related ecological processes essential for the functioning of the biosphere in all its diversity, in particular those important for food production, health and other aspects of human survival and sustainable development. In the 1980 World Conservation Strategy the main ecosystems involved are referred to as "life-support systems".

The most important of those life-support systems are agricultural systems, forests and coastal and fresh water systems. Agricultural systems or land suitable for agricultural purposes is a relatively scarce natural resource which is of crucial importance for the world's production of food. Forests are of vital importance for people because they supply timber and other products, and because they regulate local and regional climates and retain soil cover on site and protect areas downstream from excessive floods and other harmful fluctuations in streamflow. Coastal wetlands and shallows (especially estuaries and mangrove forests) provide nutrients and nurseries for most of the world's fisheries. Coral reefs also provide habitats for the fish. Similarly many fresh water wetlands and flood plains support important inland fisheries, while flood plain agriculture has long relied on the regular supply of nutrients by flood waters.

The life-support systems just mentioned may be adversely affected in many ways. Agricultural areas may be lost by being built on or by the erosion of the soil as a result of poorly managed human activities. Such degradation of the land may also involve the destruction of habitats of beneficial insects and other animals, such as crop pollinators and the predators and parasites of pests. Deforestation and overgrazing may lead to loss of soil, silting up of rivers, hydroelectric facilities or irrigation systems or may give rise to excessive flooding. Coastal or fresh water systems may be adversely affected by habitat destruction or pollution.

It follows from the foregoing that protection of the life-support systems and the related essential ecological processes requires rational planning and allocation of uses and high quality management of those uses designed to prevent, inter alia, degradation of soil and habitats, uncontrolled deforestation and pollution.

Paragraph (b) of the present article contains a special obligation for States to maintain maximum genetic diversity. As postulated in the 1980 World Conservation Strategy, preservation of genetic or biological diversity is not only imperative on ethical grounds, but also:

> "[A] matter of insurance and investment—necessary to sustain and improve agricultural, forestry and fisheries production, to keep open future options, as a buffer against harmful environmental change, and as the raw material for much scientific and industrial innovation."

Indeed the preservation of the genetic material contained in both domesticated or wild plants and animals is essential for breeding programmes designed to improve yields, nutritional quality, flavour, durability, pest and disease resistance or responsiveness to different soils and climates. Preservation of genetic diversity is essential for the supply of food, as well as for the production of medicines or other pharmaceutical products. Many species, moreover, are useful for scientific research, whether as experimental material or as providers of clues to technical innovations.

In order to preserve maximum biological diversity measures must be taken against destruction of habitats, over-exploitation of living resources and adverse effects on native species caused by the introduction of exotic species. Apart from these measures of on-site preservation, measures of off-site preservation must be taken in the form of timely collection of genetic material and its protection in banks, or plantations, zoos, botanic gardens, and aquaria.

Paragraph (c) obliges States to observe in the exploitation of living natural resources and ecosystems the principle of optimum sustainable yield. This means that a living natural resource or ecosystem must only be utilized in such a manner and to such an extent that benefits from those resources will be provided indefinitely. If this principle is not obeyed the resource will diminish or will even be extinguished.

Thus, in the case of aquatic animals, over-fishing must be prevented. Over-exploitation of wild plants and animals of the land or of such ecosystems as grazing lands (through overstocking or uncontrolled grazing) or forests and woodlands (through uncontrolled deforestation) must also be avoided. In order to arrive at a sustainable level of an exploited living natural resource or ecosystem it will, hence, be necessary to determine the productive capacity of the living natural resource or ecosystem concerned. It should then also be borne in mind that, in the case of a species, the productive capacity will not only depend on the biology of the species, but also on the quality of the ecosystems that support it.

It will be noted that in Paragraph (c) the concept of *optimum* sustainable yield instead of *maximum* sustainable yield has been used as a yardstick to achieve and maintain sustainable utilization of a living natural resource or ecosystem. Scientific analyses have indicated that attempts to harvest a species at the maximum sustainable yield level still entails severe risks of stock depletion as it does not allow a margin for error, lack of adequate data and/or uncertainty. Moreover, a safety margin is called for in order to reckon with important interdependences between the exploited species and other species or ecosystems of which they form a part. Thus, it is scientifically impossible for fisheries which harvest both predator species and their prey (e.g. whales and krill) to harvest both predator and prey simultaneously at the maximum sustainable yield level. In the concept of optimum sustainable yield these factors are duly taken into account.

Regulatory measures to achieve or maintain exploitation of a species at or below the optimum sustainable yield level may include restrictions of the total take, the number of persons, vessels or other units allowed to participate in the exploitation and of the times (closed seasons) and places of exploitation (protected areas). They also may include prohibitions or restrictions of the use of certain methods and equipment. Another important means to control the exploitation of certain plants or animals or parts or derivatives thereof may consist in trade and marketing restrictions. In the case of the exploitation of forests, timber companies may further be required to assume responsibility for reforestation.

To what extent have the principles laid down in the above article found support in existing international legal instruments?

In addition to treaty provisions specifically relating to transboundary environmental interferences (see the comment on Article 10) reference can in this connection first be made to treaty provisions which (also) purport to counteract *pollution* in international areas, such as the high seas and/or its subsoil, or pollution which is or may be limited to areas under national jurisdiction.

Treaty provisions purporting to protect *marine* waters are to be found, inter alia, in:

1969 Bonn Agreement for Co-operation in Dealing with Water Pollution of the North Sea by Oil;

1972 Oslo Convention for the Prevention of Marine Pollution by Dumping from Ships and Aircraft;

1972 Convention on the Prevention of Marine Pollution by Dumping of Wastes and Other Matter;

1973 London International Convention for the Prevention of Pollution from Ships;

1974 Helsinki Convention for the Protection of the Marine Environment of the Baltic Sea Area;

1976 Barcelona Convention for the Mediterranean Sea;

1978 Kuwait Regional Convention;

1981 Abidjan Convention for the West and Central African Region;

1982 Jeddah Regional Convention;

1982 UN Law of the Sea Convention (mainly Part XII); and

1983 Cartagena de Indias Convention for the Wider Caribbean Region.

Treaty provisions purporting to protect (also) *waters other than marine waters* against pollution are, in addition to those specifically relating to transboundary pollution (see the comment on Article 10), to be found in the 1968

European Agreement on the Restriction of the Use of Certain Detergents in Washing and Cleaning Products, or in the 1968 African Convention on the Conservation of Nature and Natural Resources (Article 5(1)(4)). Also relevant in this connection are certain EEC Council directives, in particular, the 1976 EEC Council Directive on Pollution Caused by Certain Dangerous Substances Discharged into the Aquatic Environment of the Community; and certain directives which lay down water quality objectives for surface water intended for the abstraction of drinking, for bathing water, for fresh waters needing protection or improvement in order to support fish life and for water favourable for the culture of shell fish.

While the 1979 ECE Convention on Long-Range Transboundary Air Pollution is mainly concerned with transboundary air pollution, certain EEC Council directives are not, viz., the 1975 EEC Council Directive relating to the Sulphur Content of Gas Oils; 1980 EEC Council Directive on Air Quality Limit Values and Guide Values for Sulphur Dioxide and Suspended Particulates; and 1982 EEC Council Directive on Air Quality Limit Value for Lead.

Dealing generally with activities likely to cause pollution of the air, soil, fresh water, or the marine environment or likely to cause other forms of environmental degradation is the 1985 ASEAN Agreement on the Conservation of Nature and Natural Resources (Articles 10 and 11).

Certain species or ecosystems also may be detrimentally affected by the accidental or deliberate *introduction of alien species*. Fortunately there is a growing tendency in international conservation agreements to provide for the control of the introduction of such species. Relevant examples are the 1976 Apia Convention on Conservation of Nature in the South Pacific and the 1979 Berne Convention on the Conservation of European Wildlife and Natural Habitats (Article 11 (2)(b)). Indicative of this trend also is Article 196 of the 1982 UN Law of the Sea Convention which provides:

"States shall take all necessary measures to prevent, reduce and control . . . the intentional or accidental introduction of species, alien or new, to a particular part of the marine environment, which may cause significant and harmful changes thereto."

Many international agreements also purport to protect the habitats of species by obliging the parties to set up *protected areas*. Noteworthy examples are:

1940 Washington Convention on Nature Protection and Wild Life Preservation in the Western Hemisphere;
1950 Paris International Convention for the Protection of Birds;

1968 African Convention on the Conservation of Nature and Natural Resources;

1971 Ramsar Convention on Wetlands of International Importance, Especially as Water Fowl Habitat;

1972 London Convention for the Conservation of Antarctic Seals;

1972 Paris Convention concerning the Protection of World Cultural and Natural Heritage; and

1976 Apia Convention on Conservation of Nature in the South Pacific.

It should be noted that, as in various other international agreements already mentioned above, general protection of the habitats of wild fauna and flora is envisaged in the 1979 Berne Convention on the Conservation of European Wildlife and Natural Habitats.

A considerable number of international agreements have been entered into by States obliging them to take measures to prevent *over-exploitation of living natural resources*.

Having regard to the principle of freedom of fishing on the high seas, it is understandable that the need to conclude such agreements arose first of all with respect to the exploitation of the living resources of the high seas. Thus, relatively early, various fisheries agreements were concluded in order to conserve *particular (groups of) species*. Reference may be made to, e.g.:

1911 Convention for the Preservation and Protection of Fur Seals (followed by a second convention in 1957), which outlawed pelagic sealing of the North Pacific fur seals;

1923 Convention for the Preservation of the Halibut Fishery of the Northern Pacific Ocean and the Bering Sea concluded between the United States and Canada (followed by a second convention in 1930, a third convention in 1937 and a fourth convention in 1953); and

1931 and 1946 International Conventions for the Regulation of Whaling.

Other conventions were concluded in order to manage fisheries *in specific areas* such as the 1946 London Convention for the Regulation of the Meshes of Fishing Nets and the Size Limits of Fish (followed by a second convention in 1959, see *infra*), which applied to all the waters of the North-East Atlantic or the 1949 Washington International Convention for the North-West Atlantic Fisheries.

The 1958 UN Convention on Fishing and Conservation of the Living Resources of the High Seas obliged States to adopt, or to co-operate with other States in adopting, such measures for their respective nationals as would be necessary for the conservation of the living resources of the high seas. It is true that the convention defined "conservation of the living resources of the high seas" as "the aggregate of the measures rendering possible the *optimum* sustainable yield from those resources . . ." (Article 2, emphasis added), but it is generally agreed that this notion was meant to be equal, or at least very similar, to the concept of maximum sustainable yield. The convention simply provided a very general framework for the conclusion of subsequent more limited, but also more detailed fisheries agreements. It also provided that access of new entrants to a regulated existing fishery was contingent upon the acceptance by the entrants of the conservation measures taken in the area of that fishery by the State or States that were engaged in fishing in that area previously.

After the conclusion of the 1958 UN Convention a number of new fisheries agreements were concluded. Most of these agreements applied to *specific areas of the ocean* where fishing fleets of different nations were exploiting the same stocks of fish thus giving rise to a severe risk of overfishing. Reference can be made to, e.g.:

1959 London North-East Atlantic Fisheries Convention, which replaced the 1946 London Convention for the Regulation of the Meshes of Fishing Nets and the Size Limits of Fish;

1959 Varna Convention concerning Fishing in the Black Sea;

1969 Rome Convention on the Conservation of the Living Resources of the South-East Atlantic;

1973 Gdansk Convention on Fishing and Conservation of the Living Resources in the Baltic Sea and the Belts.

Certain new agreements purported to conserve *particular species* in certain marine areas, e.g. the 1966 Rio de Janeiro International Convention for the Conservation of Atlantic Tunas, and with respect to marine mammals:

1963 Washington Protocol to the 1949 Washington International Convention for the North-West Atlantic Fisheries, extending the provisions of the convention to harp and hooded seals;

1972 London Convention for the Conservation of Antarctic seals;

1973 Oslo Agreement on the Conservation of Polar Bears; and

1976 Washington Convention on the Conservation of North Pacific Fur Seals.

Most of these agreements referred to the objectives of an "optimum sustainable yield", "maximum sustainable catch" or "maximum sustainable productivity", but, in consequence of the 1958 UN Convention, meant by this notion nothing else than the concept of the maximum sustainable yield.

Implementation of these agreements hence entailed a great danger of over-exploitation of the natural resources concerned.

Under the 1982 UN Law of the Sea Convention coastal States are entitled to an exclusive economic zone (EEZ) extending to a maximum of 200 nautical miles from the baselines from which the breadth of the territorial sea is measured. Within the EEZ the coastal State has sovereign rights, inter alia, for the purpose of exploring and exploiting, conserving and managing the natural resources, and jurisdiction with regard to, inter alia, marine scientific research and the protection and preservation of the marine environment (Article 56). Thus, a considerable extension of the area of national jurisdiction of the coastal State has taken place, covering now practically all of the world's presently exploited marine living resources as against a negligible percentage previously.

A result of the considerable extension of the national jurisdiction of the coastal States under the 1982 UN Law of the Sea Convention is that many of the fisheries conventions referred to earlier had to be renegotiated and that in some of the renegotiated agreements fishery commissions are no longer entitled to regulate fishing in those parts of the convention area that are now included in the EEZ of their members.

The sovereign rights of the coastal State are somewhat limited in that the coastal State must determine the allowable catch for the living resources in its EEZ (Article 61(1)) and its own capacity to harvest that allowable catch (Article 62(1)). If it does not have the capacity to harvest the entire allowable catch by itself, it must give other States access to the surplus of the allowable catch.

The reverse side of the considerable increase in national jurisdiction of the coastal States over the marine living resources is that they have now an obligation to "ensure through proper conservation and management measures that the maintenance of the living resources in the exclusive economic zone is not endangered by overexploitation" and that they must co-operate with other States in the conservation and management of shared stocks (Article 61(2)). Article 61(3) of the 1982 UN Law of the Sea Convention provides on this point in particular:

"3. Such measures shall also be designed to maintain or restore populations of harvested species at levels which can produce the maximum sustainable yield, as qualified by relevant environmental and economic factors, including the economic needs of coastal fishing communities and the special requirements of developing States, and taking into account fishing patterns, the interdependence of stocks and any generally recommended international minimum standards, whether subregional, regional or global."

Similar obligations have been imposed on States in respect of the conservation of the living resources of the high seas (see Article 119(a)). It will be noted that in respect of the growing criticism expressed in recent years against the concept of maximum sustainable yield, the 1982 UN Law of the Sea Convention has retained the concept as a basis for conservation and management of living resources. It is true that this concept is qualified by relevant environmental and economic factors, but it must be expected that these will more or less neutralize one another. Taking further into account that States enjoy considerable discretion in the establishment of the allowable catch, it may be expected that in many cases over-exploitation will take place.

While practically all of the treaties mentioned above concerned the exploitation of living resources in marine waters, restrictions on the exploitation of living resources in other areas are to be found in certain other treaties. Fairly elaborate provisions are, e.g. to be found in respect of the protection of soil, water, flora and fauna in the 1968 African Convention on the Conservation of Nature and Natural Resources (Articles 4–8).

Our survey of relevant international instruments concerning exploitation of living resources indicates that the *maximum* sustainable yield concept still prevails. However, for sound reasons of environmental protection the notion of *optimum* sustainable yield as described above has been retained in Paragraph (c) of the present article.

As we have already noted over-exploitation of species may also be avoided or checked by prohibiting or regulating the trade of endangered plants or animals and/or parts or derivatives thereof. A rather early example of such a regulation is to be found in:

Article 9 of the 1940 Washington Convention on Nature Protection and Wild Life Preservation in the Western Hemisphere;
Articles 3 and 4 of the 1950 Paris International Convention for the Protection of Birds; or
Article 5 of the 1973 Oslo Agreement on the Conservation of Polar Bears.

Highly important, in this connection, inter alia, because of its broad scope and the great number of parties, is the 1973 Washington Convention on International Trade in Endangered Species of Wild Fauna and Flora.

The principles laid down in the present article have not only found more or less substantial support in many international agreements, but also in numerous resolutions adopted by international organizations or at international conferences. It is not possible to discuss these resolutions here *in extenso* or even to mention all of them. It must, therefore, suffice to note that, in addition to the various EEC directives which have been mentioned above and those especially concerning transboundary natural resources and environmental interferences mentioned elsewhere, more or less substantial support for the principles laid down in the present article may also be found, for example, in:

1972 UN Declaration on the Human Environment (see especially Principles 2–7, 17);

certain recommendations made during the 1972 UN Conference on the Human Environment (see especially Recommendations 38 et seq., 71, 86, 92);

various resolutions adopted by the OECD Council of Ministers (see e.g. OECD Council Recommendations C(73) 172(Final), C(74)219, C(74)221, C(78)4(Final), C(78)73(Final), or OECD Council Decision C(73)1(Final).

Support is also to be found in various recommendations adopted by the Committee of Ministers of the Council of Europe, the 1977 UN Mar del Plata Water Conference and, of course, to a very large extent in UNGA Resolution No. 37/7 of 28 October 1982, which proclaimed the World Charter for Nature, or in the 1982 UNEP Gov. Council Nairobi Declaration.

Article 4
Environmental standards and monitoring

States shall:

(a) establish specific environmental standards, in particular environmental quality standards, emission standards, technological standards and product standards, aimed at preventing or abating interferences with natural resources or the environment;

(b) establish systems for the collection and dissemination of data and regular observation of natural resources and the environment in order to permit adequate planning of the use of natural resources and the environment, to permit early detection of interferences with

natural resources or the environment and ensure timely intervention, and to facilitate the evaluation of conservation policies and methods.

Comment

(a) States shall establish specific environmental standards, i.e. concrete numerical or technical standards aimed at preventing or abating detrimental interferences with natural resources or the environment. These specific environmental standards are an important tool for the conservation of natural resources and the environment as they provide usually concrete yardsticks for both users and preservers of natural resources and/or the environment, taking into account local, regional or sometimes even global conditions and preferred functions of the natural resources or environment concerned. These specific environmental standards may take various forms.

They may be so-called environmental quality standards, i.e. standards which prescribe the minimum or maximum permissible level of a certain substance or physical effect in a given part of the environment such as the soil, water or air space, which at a given moment must be met, or as the case may be, must not be exceeded.

There are also so-called emission (or discharge) standards which prescribe the maximum permissible release of a certain pollutant from a given source (e.g. a dwelling, a certain type of industry, a means of transport or a municipal purification plant) to a certain part of the environment under specified conditions.

So-called technological standards lay down prescriptions for technologies or operations (e.g. production, storage or transport equipment, facilities and/or operations) which may involve the release of pollutants.

Product standards lay down specific technical conditions regarding the composition of certain products which may otherwise unduly affect the quality of certain natural resources and/or the environment.

In principle technological standards, product standards and/or emission standards ought to be set in such a way that environmental quality standards are attained or maintained.

Specific environmental quality standards have, e.g. been envisaged in such international or regional instruments as the 1976 EEC Council Directive on Pollution Caused by Certain Dangerous Substances Discharged into the Aquatic Environment of the Community (Articles 6 and 7).

Important also are the standards concerning radioactive contamination of water and air established by the Euratom Council of Ministers under Article 30 et seq. of the 1957 Treaty Establishing the European Atomic Energy

Community, or in certain EEC directives which purport to protect surface water intended for the abstraction of drinking water, for bathing, for fresh water needing protection or improvement in order to support fish life and for the culture of shell fish.

Specific water quality standards also have been recommended by the Conference of Heads of Water Management Bodies of the Council of Mutual Economic Assistance (CMEA). The adoption of such standards was further recommended in Recommendation 39(p) adopted by the 1977 UN Mar del Plata Water Conference.

With regard to air pollution reference may be made to the 1980 EEC Council Directive on Air Quality Limit Values and Guide Values for Sulphur Dioxide and Suspended Particulates and 1982 EEC Council Directive on Air Quality Limit Value for Lead.

The formulation of specific emission (or discharge) standards at the national level has been envisaged in the 1976 EEC Council Directive on Pollution Caused by Certain Dangerous Substances Discharged into the Aquatic Environment of the Community and so-called limit values for such emission standards have been adopted in certain implementing EEC directives concerning specific dangerous substances such as, e.g. mercury or cadmium. A separate framework EEC directive envisages the adoption at the national level of emission standards for groundwater. Specific emission standards for certain air pollutants emitted by vehicles have been adopted by the EEC in the past (see, e.g. the 1970 EEC Directive on the Approximation of the Laws of the Member States relating to Measures to be Taken against Air Pollution by Gases from Positive-Ignition Engines of Motor Vehicles) while new and more stringent ones are at present the subject of discussion and negotiation in the EEC Council of Ministers.

Outside the EEC framework reference may be made, e.g. to the 1979 OECD Council Recommendation C(79)117 on Coal and the Environment (esp. Recommendation III); 1974 OECD Council Recommendation C(74)217 on Noise Prevention and Abatement; or 1978 OECD Council Recommendation C(78)73 (Final) on Noise Abatement Policies.

Specific technological standards are recommended, e.g. in UNGA Resolution No. 37/7 of 28 October 1982 on the World Charter for Nature (Article 21) and imposed by the 1973 OECD Decision C(73)1(Final) on Protection of the Environment by Control of Polychlorinated Biphenyls. They are also to be found in IMO rules concerning the construction and equipment of ships carrying dangerous chemicals in bulk or in IAEA regulations concerning the safe operation of nuclear power plants or the safe transport of radioactive materials, etc.

Finally, an example of an internationally agreed product standard for the protection of water is to be found in the 1968 European Agreement on the Restriction of the Use of Certain Detergents in Washing and Cleaning Products. This agreement provides that the Parties must accept measures as effective as possible to ensure that:

"a. In their respective territories washing or cleaning products containing one or more synthetic detergents are not put on the market unless the detergents in the product considered are, as a whole, at least eighty per cent susceptible to biological degradation; . . .".

A similar prescription is to be found in the 1973 EEC Council Directive on the Approximation of the Laws of the Member States relating to Detergents (requiring biodegradability of at least 90 per cent). Other EEC directives lay down rules concerning the composition of certain fuels (viz. concerning the sulphur content of gas oils or the content of lead in motor vehicle petrol).

None of the examples of specific environmental standards mentioned above purport to deal specifically with transboundary natural resources or environmental interferences. Examples of standards which specifically concern transboundary natural resources or environmental interferences have been dealt with in the comment on Article 18, Paragraph (c).

(b) States shall establish systems for the collection and dissemination of data and regular observation of natural resources and the environment in order to permit adequate planning of the use of natural resources and the environment, to permit early detection of interferences with natural resources or the environment and ensure timely intervention, and to facilitate the evaluation of conservation policies and methods.

Support for the establishment of systems for the collection and dissemination of data and regular observation of natural resources and the environment for one or more of the purposes already mentioned is to be found:

in various recommendations adopted at the 1972 UN Conference on the Human Environment (see, e.g. Recommendations 76 and 87);
at the 1977 UN Mar del Plata Water Conference (see, e.g. Recommendation 1 et seq. and Resolution I);
1981 UNEP Conclusions of the Study on the Legal Aspects concerning the Environment related to Offshore Mining and Drilling within the Limits of National Jurisdiction (Conclusions 11–15);
UNGA Resolution No. 37/7 on the World Charter for Nature (Article 19);
1974 OECD Recommendation C(74)219 on Measures Required for Further Air Pollution Control;

1974 OECD Recommendation C(77)97(Final) on Guidelines in respect of
Procedures and Requirements for Anticipating the Effects of Chemicals on
Man and in the Environment (Annex I Paragraphs 30–31); or

1978 OECD Council Recommendation C(78)4(Final) on Water Management
Policies and Instruments (Paragraph 8).

Support for Paragraph (b) may also be found in a growing number of
international agreements, some of which may be mentioned by way of
example, viz.:

1968 African Convention on the Conservation of Nature and Natural
Resources (Article 5(1)(i));

1976 Barcelona Convention for the Mediterranean Sea (Article 10);

1978 Kuwait Regional Convention (Article 10);

1981 Abidjan Convention for the West and Central African Region (Article
14);

1982 UN Law of the Sea Convention (Articles 204 and 205);

1983 Cartagena de Indias Convention for the Wider Caribbean Region; and

1985 ASEAN Agreement on the Conservation of Nature and Natural
Resources.

For relevant international legal instruments more specifically relating to
transboundary natural resources and environmental interferences reference is
made to the comment on Article 18, Paragraph (a).

Article 5
Assessment of planned activities

**States planning to carry out or permit activities which may
significantly affect a natural resource or the environment shall make or
require an assessment of their effects before carrying out or permitting
the planned activities.**

Comment

The duty provided for in the principle formulated above is of vital importance in order to prevent significant interferences with natural resources or
the environment. It requires States, before commitments or irrevocable
decisions are made, to assess or require the assessment of the nature and
extent of effects of planned activities which may significantly affect natural
resources or the environment.

Growing support for the duty of States to assess or require the assessment of the environmental impact of planned activities is to be found in a number of recent treaties. A good example is Article 14(1) of the 1985 ASEAN Agreement on the Conservation of Nature and Natural Resources which provides:

"The Contracting Parties undertake that proposals for any activity which may significantly affect the natural environment shall as far as possible be subjected to an assessment of their consequences before they are adopted, and they shall take into consideration the results of their assessment in their decision-making process."

Articles 19(2)(c) and 20(3)(a) of the ASEAN Agreement concern more specifically the assessment of the environmental impact of projects or activities which affect shared natural resources or produce transboundary environmental effects (see the comment on Article 16).

Reference should also be made to Article 206 of the 1982 UN Law of the Sea Convention which provides:

"When States have reasonable grounds for believing that planned activities under their jurisdiction or control may cause substantial pollution of or significant and harmful changes to the marine environment, they shall, as far as practicable, assess the potential effects of such activities on the marine environment and shall communicate reports of the results of such assessments [at appropriate intervals to the competent international organizations, which should make them available to all States]."

Similar provisions are to be found in various regional treaties concerning pollution of the marine environment, viz.:

1978 Kuwait Regional Convention (Article 11);
1981 Abidjan Convention for the West and Central African Region (Article 13);
1981 Lima Convention for the Coastal Area of the South-East Pacific (Article 8);
1982 Jeddah Regional Convention (Article 11; see also Chapter I of the Action Plan); and
1983 Cartagena de Indias Convention for the Wider Caribbean Region (Article 12).

While some of these treaties do not cover inland waters, they all purport to protect the marine environment regardless of whether or not the potential effects of planned activities will be felt only within the territorial waters of the States concerned.

The treaties just mentioned merely lay down an obligation in principle for States to make or require the assessment of the potential detrimental effects of planned activities on the use of natural resources or on the environment and do not give any information on *how* the assessment is to take place in practice. On this point States may be guided by certain conclusions relating to environmental impact assessments contained in Chapter C of the 1981 UNEP Conclusions of the Study on the Legal Aspects concerning the Environment related to Offshore Mining and Drilling within the Limits of National Jurisdiction which have been reached by the UNEP Working Group of Experts on Environmental Law and which were subsequently endorsed by the UN General Assembly in its Resolution No. 37/217 of 24 March 1983 on International Co-operation in the Field of the Environment. According to Conclusion No. 8:

> "The [environmental impact] assessment should cover the effects of operations on the environment, wherever such effects may occur. It should when deemed appropriate contain the following:
> (a) a description of the geographical boundaries of the area within which the operations are to be carried out;
> (b) a description of the initial ecological state of the area;
> (c) an indication of the nature, aims and scope of the proposed operations;
> (d) a description of the methods, installations and other means to be used;
> (e) a description of the foreseeable direct and indirect long-term and short-term effects of the operations on the environment, including fauna, flora and the ecological balance;
> (f) a statement setting out the measures proposed to reduce to the minimum the risk of damage to the environment from carrying out the operations and, in addition, possible alternatives to such measures;
> (g) an indication of the measures to be taken for the protection of the environment from pollution and other adverse effects during and at the end of the proposed operations;
> (h) a brief summary of the assessment that may be easily understood by a layman."

Considerable support for the principle formulated above is also to be found in resolutions of intergovernmental organizations. Reference should be made to:

UNGA Resolution No. 37/7 of 28 October 1982 on the World Charter for Nature (Articles 11 and 16; see for the text of Article 16 the comment on Article 6);

1981 Antarctic Treaty Consultative Meeting Recommendation XI-I on Antarctic Mineral Resources (Paragraph 7);

1984 ECA Council of Ministers Resolution on Environment and Development in Africa (Paragraph 2(1));

1974 OECD Governments' Declaration on Environmental Policy (Paragraph 9); and

many recommendations adopted by the OECD Council of Ministers.

Some of those recommendations recommend environmental impact assessment more in general, viz.:

1974 OECD Council Recommendation C(74)216 on Analysis of the Environmental Consequences of Significant Public and Private Projects (Paragraph (1));

1979 OECD Council Recommendation C(79)116 on the Assessment of Projects with Significant Impact on the Environment (Paragraphs 1(1), (2) and (8)).

Other OECD Council recommendations recommend environmental impact assessment in specific contexts, viz.:

(1) the use of chemicals, see:

1974 OECD Council Recommendation C(74)215 on the Assessment of the Potential Chemical Effects of Chemicals (Paragraph 1);

1977 OECD Council Recommendation C(77)97(Final) on Guidelines in respect of Procedures and Requirements for Anticipating the Effects of Chemicals on Man and on the Environment;

(2) energy production, see:

1976 OECD Council Recommendation C(76)162(Final) on Reduction of Environmental Impacts from Energy Production and Use (Paragraph 2(5));

1979 OECD Council Recommendation C(79)117 on Coal and the Environment (Paragraph 5);

(3) development assistance projects, see:

1985 OECD Council Recommendation C(85)104 on Environmental Assessment of Development Assistance Projects and Programmes;

1986 Draft OECD Council Recommendation C(86)26 on Measures Required to Facilitate the Environmental Assessment of Development Assistance Projects and Programmes; or

(4) exports of hazardous wastes, see:

1984 OECD Council Decision-Recommendation C(83)180(Final) on Transfrontier Movements of Hazardous Waste;

1986 OECD Council Decision-Recommendation C(86)64(Final) on Exports of Hazardous Wastes from the OECD Area.

Finally reference should be made to the 1985 EEC Council Directive on the Assessment of the Effects of Certain Public and Private Projects on the Environment. This directive obliges EEC Member States to ensure the assessment of the environmental impact of public or private projects which are likely to have significant effects on the environment. The directive is of great importance because it covers an extensive and at the same time highly industrialized area of the world. Furthermore, it is of great interest because of the extent to which the obligation of the EEC Member States to ensure environmental impact assessments has been elaborated in the annexes to the directive. Thus, Annexes I and II to the directive specify the types of project which are in principle subject, or eligible to become subject, to the environmental impact assessment requirement. Moreover, Annex III specifies in detail the type of information which must be provided in the environmental impact assessment process.

Unfortunately the directive also provides for certain not unimportant exceptions. First of all, the directive does not apply to "projects the details of which are adopted by a specific act of national legislation" in order to allow Denmark to continue its own procedure of detailed parliamentary examination and approval of projects which may have significant effects on the environment. This procedure, however, includes the environmental impact assessment of proposed projects, albeit not subject to the conditions imposed by the directive.

More serious is the exception provided for in Article 2(3) of the directive which allows EEC Member States in exceptional cases and under certain conditions of a more procedural than substantive nature to exempt a specific project in whole or in part from the duty to undertake an environmental impact assessment. To this may be added the fact that under Article 4(2) of the directive the EEC Member States retain a certain discretion to determine whether the types of project listed in Annex II have such characteristics that they ought to be subject to environmental impact assessment in accordance with the directive.

In the light of the foregoing observations it may be concluded that the principle formulated above is an emerging principle of international law.

Article 6
Timely information, access and due process

States shall inform all persons in a timely manner of activities which may significantly affect their use of a natural resource or their environment and shall grant the concerned persons access to and due process in administrative and judicial proceedings.

Comment

The principle formulated above is explicitly concerned with the position of natural or legal persons. However, this does not necessarily imply that the persons concerned must be deemed to have acquired international legal personality, i.e. have become the bearers of a right under international law to demand compliance with the duty of States contained in the principle formulated above. Indeed, that principle may also be deemed to reflect a duty of the State vis-à-vis other States "merely" for the benefit of "persons" in order to protect them against infringements upon their use of a natural resource or their environment.

The principle formulated above states in fact two main duties. One duty is to inform all persons by appropriate means in time of planned or, as the case may be, already initiated activities which may significantly affect their use of a natural resource or their environment. The other duty consists in granting the persons concerned a right of access to and due process in administrative hearings concerning the granting of licences for proposed activities, enabling those persons to raise objections and to influence the conditions under which the administrative authorities may grant permission for the proposed activities. These persons should also be given a possibility to appeal to administrative courts in order to challenge the granting of a licence by the administrative authorities. According to the principle formulated above, States must also see to it that the persons concerned may have resort to a court in order to obtain an injunction and/or compensation when activities in fact significantly affect their use of a natural resource or their environment.

The principle formulated above is a fairly novel one, certainly in so far as it also comprises instances of pollution or degradation of nature occurring entirely within an area under the national jurisdiction of a State or within an area beyond the limits of national jurisdiction.

The question of access to civil or ordinary courts has to some extent been dealt with in the 1968 EC Jurisdiction and Execution of Judgments Convention and in certain conventions which impose strict liability on the operators of nuclear installations for nuclear damage caused by nuclear incidents (see the comment on Article 20). Certain other international agreements concerning access to and due process in (national or international) administrative or judicial proceedings relate specifically to transboundary interferences (see the comment on Article 20).

Support for the principle formulated above may be found in certain resolutions adopted by intergovernmental organizations or at international conferences. Reference must in the first place be made to the following provisions in UNGA Resolution No. 37/7 of 28 October 1982 on the World Charter for Nature:

> "16. All planning shall include, among its essential elements, the formulation of strategies for the conservation of nature, the establishment of ecosystems and assessments of the effects on nature of proposed policies and activities; *all of these elements shall be disclosed to the public by appropriate means in time to permit effective consultation and participation.*" (emphasis added).

> "23. All persons, in accordance with their national legislation, shall have the opportunity to participate, individually or with others, in the formulation of decisions of direct concern to their environment, and shall have access to means of redress when their environment has suffered damage or degradations."

Reference may also be made in respect of the furnishing of information to the persons concerned to Conclusions 10 and 13 of the 1981 UNEP Conclusions of the Study on the Legal Aspects concerning the Environment related to Offshore Drilling and Mining within the Limits of National Jurisdiction. Information and participation of the persons concerned has been recommended in Recommendation 54 adopted by the 1977 UN Mar del Plata Water Conference and in various policy statements made or recommendations adopted within the framework of the OECD, viz., the 1979 OECD Governments' Declaration of Anticipatory Environmental Policies (Paragraph 7); 1978 OECD Council Recommendation C(78)4(Final) on Water Management Policies and Instruments (Paragraph 10); or 1979 OECD Council Recommendation C(79)116 on the Assessment of Projects with Significant Impact on the Environment (Paragraph 5).

Particularly relevant also is the 1985 EEC Council Directive on the Assessment of the Effects of Certain Public and Private Projects on the Environment. According to this directive, Member States of the European Community are obliged to make available to the public concerned any information gathered under the directive by the environmental impact assessment of public or private projects which are likely to have significant effects on the environment. The public concerned must also be given the opportunity to express an opinion on the project before it is initiated (Article 6). When a decision has been taken the public concerned must, moreover, in principle (see the exception in Article 10(1)) be informed of the content of the decision and of any conditions attached thereto and of the reasons and considerations on which the decision is based (Article 9). (See for exceptions on the duty to carry out environmental impact assessments the comment on Article 5).

With regard to the position of natural or legal persons relating specifically to transboundary natural resources or environmental interferences, see further Article 20.

Article 7
Planning and implementation of development activities

1. States shall ensure that the conservation of natural resources and the environment is treated as an integral part of the planning and implementation of development activities. Particular attention shall be paid to environmental problems arising in developing countries and to the need to incorporate environmental considerations in all development assistance programmes.

2. States shall make available to other States, and especially to developing countries, upon their request and under agreed terms scientific and technical information and expertise, results of research programmes, training opportunities and specialized equipment and facilities which are needed by such other States to promote rational use of natural resources, and the environment or to prevent or abate interference with natural resources or the environment, in particular in cases of environmental emergencies.

Comment

Paragraph 1 of the present article sets out to state as a general principle applicable to *all* States, i.e. regardless of their stage of development, that the conservation of natural resources and the environment must be treated as an integral part of the planning and implementation of development activities. Indeed, this principle is of fundamental importance from the viewpoint of preventing—sometimes irreparable—impairment of natural resources or the environment. It is to be found, inter alia, in UNGA Resolution No. 37/7 of 28 October 1982 on the World Charter for Nature (Article 7). Article 2 of the 1985 ASEAN Agreement on the Conservation of Nature and Natural Resources states it as follows:

1. The Contracting Parties shall take all necessary measures, within the framework of the respective municipal laws, to ensure that conservation and management of natural resources are treated as an integral part of development planning at all stages and at all levels.

2. To that effect they shall, in the formulation of all development plans, give as full consideration to ecological factors as to economic and social ones.

Paragraph 1 of the present article stipulates further that particular attention shall be paid to environmental problems arising in developing countries. Indeed, the very condition of underdevelopment is likely to involve, in its own way, a great danger to the proper conservation of natural resources and the environment. In their efforts to close or at least narrow the development gap between the rich and the poor countries the developing countries may well be inclined to give secondary consideration to environmental concerns. Irrational use of natural resources or environmental degradation will, moreover, not only be caused by a lack of capital making it difficult to finance the facilities or personnel required to cope with environmental problems, but also by a lack of relevant scientific and technological know-how. Poverty and underdevelopment may, thus, together with certain natural phenomena such as poor soil, drought and harmful insects lead to such well-known third world problems as desertification, urbanization, deforestation and soil degradation.

The nefarious impact of poverty and underdevelopment on the conservation of natural resources and the environment is now increasingly realized by both developing and developed countries. At the same time there is also a growing awareness that irrational use of natural resources and degradation of the environment which is the result of poverty and underdevelopment will, in its turn, be a formidable obstacle to sustainable development itself. Hence, in the long run, conservation of natural resources and the environment on the one hand, and economic and social development on the other, are not incompatible but mutually re-inforcing goals. As noted in the Preamble of the 1985 ASEAN Agreement on the Conservation of Nature and Natural Resources:

"[T]he interrelationship between conservation and socio-economic development implies both that conservation is necessary to ensure sustainability of development, and that socio-economic development is necessary for the achievement of conservation on a lasting basis".

The same awareness is to be noted on the part of donors of development assistance, i.e. in the 1980 Declaration of Environmental Policies and Procedures relating to Economic Development adopted by the African Development Bank, the Arab Bank for Economic Development in Africa, the Asian Development Bank, the World Bank, the Commission of the European Community, the OAS, UNDP and UNEP (hereinafter: 1980 Declaration of Environmental Policies and Economic Development).

Hence Paragraph 1 of the above article clearly also purports to ensure that development assistance programmes are compatible with the need to conserve natural resources and the environment. Support for this aspect of Paragraph 1 is to be found, inter alia, in 1972 UN Declaration on the Human Environment (Principles 13 and 14); the International Development Strategy for the Third United Nations Development Decade (Paragraphs 156–158) adopted by UNGA Resolution No. 35/56 of 5 December 1980, and UNGA Resolution No. 37/7 of 28 October 1982 on the World Charter for Nature. Reference should further be made to certain international agreements, viz., the 1968 African Convention on the Conservation of Nature and Natural Resources (Article 14(1), (2)), and the 1985 ASEAN Agreement (Article 2(1), (2) mentioned above). These instruments amply indicate that this aspect of Paragraph 1 is also fully recognized by the developing countries themselves.

It is crucial that developed countries and international development assistance institutions make their own contribution to the implementation of this aspect of Paragraph 1. Important guidelines to that effect have been adopted in the above-mentioned 1980 Declaration of Environmental Policies and Economic Development and the 1985 OECD Council Recommendation C(85)104 on Environmental Assessment and Development Assistance Projects and Programmes. As the title indicates, the latter recommendation deals basically only with the environmental impact assessment of development assistance activities. However, in the light of the Bhopal catastrophe it is reassuring to see that "where dangerous substances or processes are involved" OECD Member States also are recommended to ensure that "they . . . continue to seek ways to promote the integration of the best techniques of prevention and protection and the best manufacturing processes in projects in which they and their industrial enterprises are involved".

Environmental impact assessment also is sometimes prescribed by national legislation in respect of (development) activities carried out abroad with the public support, financial or other, of the legislating State concerned.

Noteworthy in this connection is Section 102(2)(c) of the US National Environmental Policy Act, 42 USC Section 4321 et seq., which has been interpreted to require the preparation of an environmental impact statement whenever federal actions would have significant environmental impacts on the United States, on global resources, *or on foreign countries*. See, e.g. the US court decisions in *Wilderness Society* v. *Morton* (463 G. 2d 1261 (D.C. Cir. 1972)) concerning the construction of the Trans-Alaska Pipeline in Canada and in *Sierra Club et al.* v. *Coleman et al.* (405 F. Supp. 53 (D.C. Cir. 1975)) concerning the construction of the Darien Gap Highway through Panama and Colombia (see 14 ILM 1976 p. 1425, 15 ILM 1976 p. 1417 and also p. 1426). The preparation of these environmental impact statements is not intended to impose United States requirements on foreign countries, but to provide useful information on the foreseeable environmental consequences of projected activities to agencies of both the United States and the country in which the activities are to take place.

According to Paragraph 2 of the present article, States shall make available to other States and especially to developing countries upon their request and under agreed terms scientific and technical information and expertise, results of research programmes, training opportunities and specialized equipment and facilities which are needed by such other States to promote rational use of natural resources and the environment or to prevent or abate interference with natural resources or the environment, in particular in cases of environmental emergencies.

Support for Paragraph 2 can in part be found, for instance, in:

1972 Agreement on Co-operation in the Field of Environmental Protection concluded between the United States and the USSR (esp. Article 3) and in

1974 Agreement on Co-operation in Environmental Affairs concluded between the United States and the Federal Republic of Germany (esp. Article 3);

UNGA Resolution No. 2849 of 20 December 1971 concerning Development and Environment;

1972 UN Declaration on the Human Environment (especially Principles 9 and 12);

1980 Declaration of Environmental Policies and Economic Development; and

International Development Strategy for the Third United Nations Development Decade (Paragraphs 156–158) adopted by UNGA Resolution No. 35/56 of 5 December 1980.

Considerable additional support for Paragraph 2 is further to be found in Article 202 of the 1982 UN Law of the Sea Convention concerning scientific and technical assistance to developing countries, which is quoted in full below because of its particularly specific and illustrative character.

"States shall, directly or through competent international organizations:
(a) promote programmes of scientific, educational, technical and other assistance to developing States for the protection and preservation of the marine environment and the prevention, reduction and control of marine pollution. Such assistance shall include, inter alia:
(i) training of their scientific and technical personnel;
(ii) facilitating their participation in relevant international programmes;
(iii) supplying them with necessary equipment and facilities;
(iv) enhancing their capacity to manufacture such equipment;
(v) advice on and developing facilities for research, monitoring, educational and other programmes;
(b) provide appropriate assistance, especially to developing States, for the minimization of the effects of major incidents which may cause serious pollution of the marine environment;
(c) provide appropriate assistance, especially to developing States, concerning the preparation of environmental assessments."

Article 8
General obligation to co-operate

States shall co-operate in good faith with other States or through competent international organizations in the implementation of the provisions of the preceding articles.

Comment

The present article lays down the basic obligation that States shall not merely act individually, but, where appropriate, also co-operate with other States or through competent international organizations to implement the provisions of the preceding articles. The necessity for States to co-operate with one another or through competent international organizations to that effect has been expressed in numerous international legal instruments. Thus, Principle 24 of the 1972 UN Declaration on the Human Environment provides:

"International matters concerning the protection and improvement of the environment should be handled in a co-operative spirit by all countries, big or small, on an equal footing. Co-operation through multilateral or bilateral arrangements or other appropriate means is essential to effectively control, prevent, reduce and eliminate adverse environmental effects resulting from activities conducted in all spheres, in such a way that due account is taken of the sovereignty and interests of all States."

Reference may also be made to the following:

UNGA No. 2995 of 15 December 1972 on Co-operation between States in the Field of Environment: (*"Bearing in mind* that, in exercising their sovereignty over their natural resources, States must seek, through effective bilateral and multilateral co-operation or through regional machinery, to preserve and improve the environment, . . .");
UNGA Resolution No. 37/7 of 28 October 1982 on the World Charter for Nature (Article 21);
1982 UNEP Gov. Council Nairobi Declaration (Article 10); or
1979 OECD Governments' Declaration of Anticipatory Environmental Policies (Paragraph 10).

A duty to co-operate is further to be found in many international agreements such as the 1982 UN Law of the Sea Convention (Article 197 et seq.) or most of the fisheries conventions or marine pollution conventions mentioned in the comment on Article 3. Still other examples are given below.

The obligation to co-operate in principle pertains to all elements of the obligations laid down in the preceding articles. No particular form of co-operation is recommended as the proper form of co-operation can only be decided after careful consideration of a great variety of factors such as the subject-matter of the co-operation, the geographical area to be covered, the need for short- or long-term or for incidental or institutionalized co-operation.

Thus the co-operation may be based on a bilateral agreement such as, e.g. the 1972 Agreement concluded between the United States and the USSR on Co-operation in the Field of Environmental Protection, or 1974 Agreement concluded between the United States and the Federal Republic of Germany on Co-operation in Environmental Affairs, or on a multilateral agreement such as, e.g. the 1968 African Convention on the Conservation of Nature and Natural Resources (Article 16), or 1985 ASEAN Agreement on the Conservation of Nature and Natural Resources (Articles 1 and 8).

If institutionalized, the co-operation may again assume many forms. States may co-operate within the framework of an international commission especially established for the purpose. Examples are:

Baltic Marine Environment Commission which was established under the 1974 Helsinki Convention for the Protection of the Marine Environment of the Baltic Sea Area (Article 12 et seq.);

Paris Commission established under the 1974 Paris Convention for the Prevention of Marine Pollution from Land-Based Sources (Article 15 et seq.);

Amazonean Co-operation Council envisaged in the 1978 Brasilia Treaty for Amazonian Co-operation (Article 21);

Standing Committee envisaged in the 1979 Berne Convention on the Conservation of European Wildlife and Natural Habitats (Article 13 et seq.); or

fisheries commissions established under many of the fisheries conventions mentioned in the comment on Article 3.

Sometimes a new organization is established with several organs such as the Regional Organization for the Protection of the Marine Environment established under the 1978 Kuwait Regional Convention (Article 16 et seq.) with a Council, a Secretariat and a Judicial Commission for the Settlement of Disputes.

Other conventions, like the 1976 Barcelona Convention for the Mediterranean Sea (Articles 13 and 14) and the 1980 Athens Protocol (Article 13 et seq.) to that convention; 1981 Abidjan Convention for the West and Central African Region (Articles 16 and 17); and the 1983 Cartagena de Indias Convention for the Wider Caribbean Region (Articles 15 and 16), provide for regular meetings of the Parties and designate UNEP as responsible for carrying out various secretarial functions.

States may also choose to co-operate through one of the already existing (organs of) international or regional organizations (including many of the specialized agencies of the United Nations), such as the FAO, IAEA, ICAO, IMO, WHO, WMO, UNEP, various regional economic commissions established by the UN ECOSOC, viz., the ECE, ECLA, ESCAP and ECA, or various other regional or functional organizations such as the European Communities, Benelux, Council of Europe, CMEA or OECD.

With regard to co-operation concerning more particularly transboundary natural resources or environmental interferences, reference may be made to the comment on Article 18, Paragraph (d).

To the extent that the general obligation to co-operate laid down in Article 9 comprises a duty to prevent or abate interferences with international or transboundary natural resources or international or transboundary environmental interferences, it already may be deemed to find substantial support in existing general international law.

PRINCIPLES SPECIFICALLY CONCERNING TRANSBOUNDARY NATURAL RESOURCES AND ENVIRONMENTAL INTERFERENCES

Article 9
Reasonable and equitable use of transboundary natural resources

States shall use transboundary natural resources in a reasonable and equitable manner.

Comment

This article embodies the so-called principle of equitable utilization (or apportionment) (see on this principle further: J. G. Lammers, *Pollution of International Watercourses* (The Hague: Nijhoff, 1984), p. 364 et seq.) of a transboundary natural resource which stipulates that States are entitled to a reasonable and equitable share in the beneficial uses of a transboundary natural resource.

According to this principle no use or category of uses is inherently superior to any other use or category of uses. Whether a certain use is reasonable or not has to be determined in the light of all relevant factors in each particular case. These factors may include, inter alia, geographic, hydrologic, climatic, biologic or ecological conditions, the existing use made of the natural resource, the economic and social needs of each of the States concerned, the feasibility of alternative means—including the availability of other resources—to satisfy these needs and the possibility of compensation to one or more of the States concerned as a means of adjusting conflicts among uses. In the case of a harvested living resource the need to attain, maintain or restore the optimum sustainable yield of the resource will be an important factor. (See on this notion the comment on Article 3).

Each factor has a certain weight compared to the other factors which may vary from case to case. A use of a transboundary natural resource which is in itself reasonable and does not come into conflict with another reasonable use may continue to exist or even be expanded. However, in the case of a conflict between uses reasonable in themselves, each use must be weighed in the light of the above-mentioned factors. Although existing uses also carry considerable weight in the application of the principle of equitable utilization, this does not mean that those uses may never be encroached upon or even substantially affected. Such a use may have to be adjusted or even terminated in order to accommodate a competing incompatible use when the factors favouring its continuance are outweighed by other factors favouring its adjustment or termination. Such an adjustment or termination may or may not require compensation, depending on what is reasonable under the circumstances. It may also be that the adjustment or termination of the existing use is to take place only gradually over a reasonable period of time.

The essence of the principle of equitable utilization is that instead of laying down a norm with a more or less specific content, it rather prescribes a certain *technique* aimed at reaching an equitable *result* in each concrete case. The extremely flexible character of the principle, however, has also a disadvantage in that the principle does not provide a very concrete directive for the States concerned.

The principle of equitable use of a transboundary natural resource must be regarded as a well-established principle of international law. It has been applied in many international agreements, especially those concerning the use of the waters of international watercourses. Indeed, the implementation of the principle of equitable utilization in concrete situations usually requires negotiations between the States concerned in determining the equitable delimitation of the rights and duties of each State and any agreement reached will almost always be embodied in a treaty.

Reference may be made to:

1929 Treaty of Peace, Friendship and Arbitration concluded between Haiti and the Dominican Republic (Article 10);
1906 and 1944 Water Treaties concluded between Mexico and the United States;
1954 Convention concerning Water Economy Questions relating to the Drava concluded between Austria and Yugoslavia;
1959 Nile Waters Agreement concluded between Egypt and the Sudan;
1960 Indus Waters Treaty concluded between India and Pakistan; and
1966 Agreement Regulating the Withdrawal of Water from Lake Constance concluded between Austria, the Federal Republic of Germany and Switzerland.

It is true that the United States and India at the conclusion of the 1906 Water Treaty with Mexico and the 1960 Indus Waters Treaty with Pakistan, respectively, have made it clear that those treaties did not embody a generally recognized principle of international law. However, these States have later, in individual statements, declared themselves unambiguous proponents of the principle of equitable utilization (see: Article 5 of the 1906 Water Treaty and Article 2(2) of the 1960 Indus Waters Treaty) (see in respect of the United States: Lammers *op. cit.*, *supra* in this comment, at pp. 276–278). Thus, India in the position of an upstream State in its conflict with Bangladesh on the diversion of a part of the Ganges Waters (see: Lammers, *op. cit.*, *supra* in this comment, at p. 312 et seq.), declared in 1976 before the UNGA Special Political Committee:

> "India's view regarding the utilization of waters of an international river were similar to those held by the majority of States. When a river crossed more than one country, *each country was entitled to an equitable share of the waters of that river.* That share had to be determined by taking into account such factors as geography, the economic and social needs of the population and the availability of other resources" (emphasis added). (See: UN GAOR 31st Session Special Political Committee 21st Mtg. pp. 2–3).

Reference should further be made to two relatively recent collective statements made by States at world level. Thus, in Recommendation 51 adopted during the 1972 UN Conference on the Human Environment, States were requested to consider the principle that:

> "[T]he net benefits of hydrologic regions common to more than one national jurisdiction *are to be shared equitably* by the nations concerned" (emphasis added).

In Recommendation 91 of the Action Plan adopted by the UN Water Conference held in 1977 in Mar del Plata (Argentina) it is, moreover, declared that:

> "[I]n relation to the use, management and development of shared water resources, national policies should take into consideration the *right* of each State . . . *to equitably utilize such resources*" (emphasis added).

Recommendation 51 was adopted almost with unanimity while Recommendation 91 was adopted with consensus.

The principle of equitable utilization has further been frequently applied by the highest courts of arbitral tribunals of certain federal States (the German *Reich*, the United States, Switzerland, India) with regard to the sharing of the waters of interstate watercourses. In particular the decisions of the US Supreme Court must be deemed to have had great influence on the development of the principle in international law (see further: Lammers, *op. cit.*, *supra* in this comment, at p. 397 et seq.).

While the principle of equitable utilization may be considered as a well-established principle of international law, it should be noted that certain Latin American countries tend to follow a more stringent approach in that they require prior consent for the use of the waters of contiguous international watercourses and prohibit the use of the waters of successive international watercourses which causes appreciable damage to other riparian States (see further: Lammers, *op. cit. supra* in this comment, at p. 292 et seq.).

Reference also may be made to Recommendation 32 adopted at the 1972 UN Conference on the Human Environment which, inter alia, purports to curtail the overexploitation of migratory species. Special mention must in this connection also be made of the 1979 Bonn Convention on the Conservation of Migratory Species of Wild Animals.

The principle of equitable utilization of a transboundary natural resource has, again, in particular with regard to the use of the waters of international watercourses, found recognition in resolutions of non-governmental international organizations, in particular in 1966 ILA Helsinki Rules on the Uses of the Waters of International Rivers (see esp. Articles 4–8); 1980 ILA Belgrade Articles on the Regulation of the Flow of Water of International Watercourses (Article 6) and also, albeit less explicitly, in 1961 IIL Salzbourg Resolution on the Use of International Non-Maritime Waters (esp. Article 3).

Article 10
Prevention and abatement of a transboundary environmental interference

States shall, without prejudice to the principles laid down in Articles 11 and 12, prevent or abate any transboundary environmental interference or a significant risk thereof which causes substantial harm—i.e. harm which is not minor or insignificant.

Comment

Subject to certain qualifications to be dealt with below, Article 10 lays down the well-established basic principle governing transboundary environmental interferences, viz. that States shall prevent or abate any such interference which causes, or entails a significant risk of causing, substantial harm in an area under national jurisdiction of another State or in an area beyond the limits of national jurisdiction. The nature of the interests (possibly) affected by the interference and the nature of the interference have already been set forth in Paragraph (f) of the definition of terms which precedes these articles.

Support for the obligation not to cause substantial harm by a transboundary environmental interference is to be found in the classic statement in the Arbitral Award of the *Trail Smelter Case (United States* v. *Canada)* which reads:

> "Under the principles of international law, as well as of the law of the United States, no State has the right to use or permit the use of its territory in such a manner as to cause injury by fumes in or to the territory of another or the properties or persons therein, when the case is of serious consequence and the injury is established by clear and convincing evidence." (See: 3 Rep. of Int. Arb. Awards p. 1911 et seq., at p. 1965).

It should be noted that the obligation to prevent or abate transboundary environmental interferences does not involve a duty to prevent or abate every transboundary harm, however small. Indeed such a stringent requirement which has also been rejected in the practice of States would unduly restrict the activities of neighbouring States. Illustrative of this approach is, e.g. the provision in the 1960 Frontier Treaty concluded between the Federal Republic of Germany and the Netherlands which provides in Article 58(2)(e):

> "The Contracting Parties shall . . . take or support . . . all measures required: (e) to prevent such excessive pollution of the boundary waters as may *substantially* impair the customary use of the waters by the neighbouring State." (emphasis added).

Other examples of such an approach being taken are to be found in the 1964 Frontier Rivers Agreement concluded between Finland and the USSR (Article 4) or in the 1973 Agreement between Mexico and the United States concerning the Permanent and Definitive Solution to the International Problem of the Salinity of the Colorado River. Article 2(1) of the 1983 Agreement concluded between Mexico and the United States to Co-operate in the Solution of Environmental Problems in the Border Area expresses it as follows:

> "The Parties undertake, *to the fullest extent practical*, to adopt the appropriate measures to prevent, reduce and eliminate sources of pollution in their respective territory which affect the border area of the other" (emphasis added).

A somewhat stricter formulated obligation is to be found in Article 192(2) of the 1982 UN Law of the Sea Convention which provides:

"States shall take all measures necessary to ensure that activities under their jurisdiction or control are so conducted as not to cause damage by pollution to other States and their environment, and that pollution arising from incidents or activities under their jurisdiction or control does not spread beyond the areas where they exercise sovereign rights in accordance with this Convention."

The duty not to cause substantial—in the sense of significant or not minor—harm through a transboundary environmental interference in the area under the national jurisdiction of another State may also be deduced from the non-treaty based practice of States and from the statements made by States individually and/or collectively (see for references to this practice and these statements: Lammers, *op. cit.* in the comment on Article 9, at pp. 346–347, 374–376).

As noted, the duty not to cause substantial harm to other States through transboundary environmental interferences may be deemed to have been explicitly or implicitly accepted in many collective statements of States. Among these statements Principle 21 of the Declaration on the Human Environment adopted during the 1972 UN Conference on the Human Environment is no doubt among the most important ones. It provides:

"States have, in accordance with the Charter of the United Nations *and the principles of international law*, the sovereign right to exploit their own resources pursuant to their own environmental policies, and the responsibility to ensure that activities within their jurisdiction or control do not cause damage to the environment of other States or of areas beyond the limits of national jurisdiction." (emphasis added).

Principle 21 in fact forms a combination of two principles placed *in a parallel position*, each of these principles *taken by itself* being of a rather absolute character. However, what was apparently intended was a reconciliation or a compromise between these two principles. In its Resolution No. 2995 of 15 December 1972 on Co-operation between States in the Field of Environment the UN General Assembly, inter alia, emphasized in operative Paragraph 1:

"That, in the exploration, exploitation and development of their natural resources, States *must* not produce *significant* harmful effects in zones situated outside their national jurisdiction." (emphasis added).

In the above-quoted paragraph, the General Assembly gave further clarification as to how Principle 21 was to be interpreted, i.e. that the exercise of sovereignty over natural resources was only permissible to the extent that such exercise did not lead to *significant* extraterritorial harmful effects (see also operative Paragraph 2 of UNGA Resolution No. 2995). Principle 21 has been reaffirmed by the General Assembly in subsequent resolutions, viz., UNGA Resolution No. 3129 of 13 December 1973 on Co-operation in the Field of the Environment concerning Natural Resources Shared by Two or More States and UNGA Resolution No. 3281 of 12 December 1974 adopting the Charter of Economic Rights and Duties of States (Articles 2, 30, 32(2)).

Support for the principle formulated above may also be found in certain other collective statements of States, viz.:

Principles 3 and 6 of the 1973 EC Programme of Action on the Environment;
1974 OECD Council Recommendation C(74)224 concerning Transfrontier Pollution (Annex Title B);
1974 OECD Council Recommendation C(74)220 on the Control of Eutrophication of Waters;
1974 OECD Council Recommendation C(74)221 on Strategies for Specific Water Pollutants Control;
1975 Final Act of the Conference on Security and Co-operation in Europe;
Principle 3 of the 1978 UNEP Draft Principles of Conduct on Shared Natural Resources.

Finally, support for the principle formulated above may be found in the decision of 16 December 1983 of the District Court of Rotterdam in the *Mines Domaniales de Potasse d'Alsace case* (see 15 Neth. Yb. Int. Law 1984 Judicial Decisions No. 9.924; see also Lammers, *op. cit.*, *supra* in the comment on Article 9, at pp. 201–205).

It should be noted that the principle formulated above does not merely state that States are obliged to prevent or abate transboundary environmental interferences which *actually* cause substantial harm, but also that they are obliged to prevent or abate activities which entail a *significant risk* of causing such harm abroad. The second statement states as a matter of fact *explicitly* what must already be deemed to be *implicit* in the duty to *prevent* transboundary environmental interferences *actually* causing substantial harm and serves to exclude any misunderstanding on this point. Of course, international law does not require the prevention or abatement of *all* risk, however small, which may cause a measure of harm which may be regarded as substantial in itself. It should, however, be borne in mind that the significance of the risk does not only depend on the probability that the risk will materialize, but also on the magnitude of harm which may be caused. This means in fact that even a risk with a very low degree of probability of materialization can still be qualified as "significant" having regard to the *enormous* harm which is likely to be caused when the risk materializes. While activities creating a significant risk of causing substantial harm must in principle be prevented or abated, it may well be that, in the case of certain dangerous activities, the unlawfulness will be taken away when all possible precautionary measures have been taken to preclude the materialization of the risk *and the benefits created by the activity must be deemed to far outweigh the benefits to be obtained by eliminating the risk* which would require putting an end to the activity itself (see the following article).

Support for the view that activities causing a significant risk of a transboundary interference must in principle be prevented or abated is to be found in Principle 3 of the 1978 UNEP Draft Principles of Conduct on Shared Natural Resources which provides that States must avoid to the maximum extent possible and reduce to the minimum extent possible the adverse environmental effects of the utilization of a shared natural resource:

". . . in particular when such utilization *might*:

(a) cause damage to the environment which *could* have repercussions on the utilization of the resource by another sharing State;

(b) *threaten* the conservation of a shared renewable resource;

(c) *endanger* the health of the population of another State." (emphasis added).

The obligation formulated in the present article is not an absolute one, i.e. States cannot be deemed to have breached an international obligation *every* time they have not been able to prevent the occurrence of a transboundary environmental interference originating in their territory and causing substantial harm beyond the limits of their national jurisdiction. In fact, the obligation of States to prevent or abate a transboundary environmental interference exists only to the extent that it is *reasonably foreseeable* that substantial harm is caused, or that there is a significant risk that such harm will be caused as a result of a certain activity taking place within the area under national jurisdiction of the State of origin. In other words the obligation resting upon the State of origin is not an obligation *guaranteeing* that substantial harm will not be caused to other States, but only a due care or due diligence obligation. Thus, the State of origin can only be deemed to have breached its obligation to counteract transboundary environmental interferences when it has intentionally or negligently caused the event which had to be prevented itself or has intentionally or negligently not prevented others in the area under its national jurisdiction from causing that event or has abstained from abating it.

It means that States will not be obliged to take measures to counteract transboundary environmental interferences in circumstances which are generally recognized to preclude international wrongfulness such as, e.g. *force majeure* and fortuitous event, distress or state of necessity. On grounds similar to those which allow the invocation of a state of necessity, the duty of developing States to counteract transboundary environmental interferences may also be somewhat less stringent in that these States are not obliged to take the same sophisticated and expensive measures which developed States must take to prevent or abate transboundary environmental interferences. Support for this view could also be found in the nature of the obligation to counteract transboundary interferences—being a due care or due diligence obligation. Reference may here be made to Principle 23 of the 1972 UN Declaration on the Human Environment.

Finally, it may be noted that the nature and the extent of the measures to be taken, of course, depends on the nature and the extent of the extraterritorial harm which must be prevented or abated. Thus, in the case of pollutants with toxic, persistent and bioaccumulative characteristics more alertness, precaution and effort is required than in respect of less harmful pollutants.

Article 11
Liability for transboundary environmental interferences resulting from lawful activities

1. If one or more activities create a significant risk of substantial harm as a result of a transboundary environmental interference, and if the overall technical and socio-economic cost or loss of benefits involved in preventing or reducing such risk far exceeds in the long run the advantage which such prevention or reduction would entail, the State which carried out or permitted the activities shall ensure that compensation is provided should substantial harm occur in an area under national jurisdiction of another State or in an area beyond the limits of national jurisdiction.

2. A State shall ensure that compensation is provided for substantial harm caused by transboundary environmental interferences resulting from activities carried out or permitted by that State notwithstanding that the activities were not initially known to cause such interferences.

Comment

The provisions contained in this article constitute an exception to the basic principle laid down in Article 10.

Paragraph 1 provides that the duty of a State to prevent or abate activities which create a significant risk of substantial harm as a result of a transboundary environmental interference does not exist if the overall technical and socio-economic cost or loss of benefits involved in preventing or reducing such risk far exceeds in the long run the advantage which such prevention or reduction would entail. However, the State which carried out or permitted the activities shall ensure that compensation is provided should substantial harm occur in an area under national jurisdiction of another State or in an area beyond the limits of national jurisdiction.

The notion of "technical and socio-economic cost or loss of benefits" is to be taken in a broad sense. It may include the financial cost to be made for the taking of precautionary measures, where technically feasible, to prevent the harmful effects of the interference, but also, when such measures are not technically feasible, the entire termination or forgoing of the, in itself beneficial, activity.

It may be that the cost or loss of benefits involved so far exceeds in the long run the advantage which the prevention or reduction of the risk of substantial harm would entail that it is not warranted to make such cost or sustain such loss of benefits. The price to be paid for the right to continue with or undertake the activity, however, is a duty for the State of origin which undertakes the activity concerned itself or expressly or implicitly permits the undertaking of such an activity by private persons or entities, to ensure that compensation is provided for the substantial harm which is actually caused in the area under national jurisdiction of another State or in an area beyond the limits of national jurisdiction.

This obligation to ensure that compensation is provided constitutes an instance of strict liability *under international law*, to the extent that the State of origin is financially liable vis-à-vis the victim State for the harmful consequences of an act not prohibited under international law (see further: Lammers, *op. cit.*, *supra* in the comment on Article 9, at p. 634 et seq.).

Such liability may arise for activities which involve a risk of causing extraterritorial harm of a possibly exceptionally serious dimension, i.e. for so-called ultrahazardous activities.

Strict liability of States under international law in respect of ultrahazardous activities has been accepted in a few treaties, viz., the well-known 1972 Convention on Liability for Damage Caused by Objects Launched into Outer

Space, and, the less well-known, 1973 Treaty between Argentina and Uruguay concerning the La Plata River and its Maritime Limits (Article 51 concerning water pollution).

International State practice *en dehors* treaties shows a very varied picture and it is not yet possible to draw definite conclusions from that practice as to the (non) existence of a rule of customary international law or a principle of international law imposing strict liability under international law upon States on account of ultrahazardous activities.

The obligation laid down in Paragraph 1, however, may also be complied with by the State of origin by ensuring that those private persons or entities which conduct the ultrahazardous activities will be liable for the harmful consequences thereof vis-à-vis the victims, imposing on those persons and entities strict liability under national law. Such strict liability *under national law* has been accepted by many States in various treaties and in their national legislation or judicial decisions for certain ultrahazardous activities. In these cases strict liability is imposed on operators or owners of installations, aircrafts or vessels, that create the risk.

Reference should be made to the 1952 Rome Convention on Damage Caused by Foreign Aircraft to Third Parties on the Surface (Article 1) which deals with damage caused by civil aviation. Strict liability for harm caused by activities involving nuclear energy is to be found in the 1960 Paris Convention on Third Party Liability in the Field of Nuclear Energy, amended by the 1964 Additional Protocol and by the 1963 Brussels Convention Supplementary to the 1960 Paris Convention; 1963 Vienna Convention on Civil Liability for Nuclear Damage; and 1962 Brussels Convention on the Liability of Operators of Nuclear Ships. It is typical for the treaties concerning the peaceful use of nuclear energy that they provide for a subsidiary and supplementary liability of the installation State or flag State—that is subsidiary and supplementary to the primary liability of the operator or owner of the installation or vessel—to guarantee the indemnification of nuclear damage up to the maximum limit of liability envisaged in the treaty. Mention should also be made of the 1969 Brussels International Convention on Civil Liability for Oil Pollution Damage and the 1976 London Convention on Civil Liability for Oil Pollution Damage Resulting from Exploration for and Exploitation of Seabed Mineral Resources.

In this connection reference also should be made to Conclusion 35 of the 1981 UNEP Conclusions of the Study on the Legal Aspects concerning the Environment related to Offshore Mining and Drilling within the Limits of National Jurisdiction.

As we have already noted, many States also have accepted strict liability under national law for ultrahazardous activities in national legislation or judicial decisions (see for a survey and detailed discussion: Lammers, *op. cit.* on the comment on Article 9, at p. 644 et seq.).

Brief reference may be made here to the French case law based on Article 1384(1) of the French Civil Code imposing strict liability *in general* for harm caused "by things that one has under one's guard". Special French legislation also imposes strict liability for harm caused by the exploitation of mines or by incidents involving nuclear installations or vessels.

Strict liability for dangerous objects or activities has been increasingly provided for in special legislation in the Federal Republic of Germany, e.g. for operators of nuclear power stations, or for operators of cables, pipelines or installations used for the transportation and delivery of electricity, gases, steam or liquids. Moreover, persons or entities who discharge substances causing pollution of rivers and lakes, the territorial sea or groundwaters, or operators of manufacturing or storage installations from which such substances escape are also held strictly liable in German law for the harm caused thereby to others.

Strict liability has also been recognized for harm caused by a so-called "source of increased danger" in Article 90 of the 1961 USSR Principles of Civil Legislation which formed the basis of Article 454 of the 1964 Civil Code of the Russian Soviet Federal Socialist Republic and of similar provisions in the codes of the other republics of the USSR.

In English common law strict liability for harm caused by ultrahazardous activities may arise under the rule developed in *Rylands* v. *Fletcher* and subsequent related cases which has, inter alia, been applied to risks created by accumulated water and gas, explosives, electricity in bulk and large quantities of noxious and inherently dangerous sewage in a sewer. Strict liability has also been imposed by certain British statutes concerning the use of nuclear energy or relating to oil pollution damage resulting from incidents at sea.

Many courts in the United States treat instances of incidental harm caused by ultrahazardous activities as so-called "absolute" nuisances involving strict liability. Other American courts treat these instances as giving rise to a separate action under either the rule in *Rylands* v. *Fletcher*, applying that rule in name or in essence, or under the related, somewhat different, rule of strict liability for abnormally dangerous activities adopted by the American Law Institute in the 1977 Restatement (Second) of the Law of Torts (Sections 519–524A).

Strict liability for damage caused by ultrahazardous objects or activities is also to be found in the legislation of certain Latin American countries, viz., in the Civil Code for the Federal District and Territories of Mexico (Article 1913) or the Civil Code of Venezuela (Article 1193).

Instances of strict liability are also be found in the legislation or case law of former possessions of France or Great Britain in Africa which are inspired by Article 1384(1) of the French Civil Court or the doctrine of *Rylands* v. *Fletcher*. Reference may further be made to the 1948 Civil Code of Egypt (Article 178); 1954 Civil Code of Libya (Article 181); new Code of Civil and Commercial Obligations of Senegal (Article 197); Civil Code of Madagascar (Articles 142 and 148); or 1960 Civil Code of Ethiopia (Articles 2069(1) and 2086).

Provisions imposing strict liability are also to be found in the legislation or case law of certain Asian countries, e.g. in:

India (doctrine of *Rylands* v. *Fletcher*);
Thailand (Article 437 of the Thai Civil and Commercial Code);
Syria (Article 179 of the Civil Code);
Kuwait (Article 19 of the 1961 Act concerning Obligations Arising from Unlawful Acts);
Iraq (Article 231 of the Civil Code);
Jordan (Article 291 of the Civil Code);
Lebanon (Article 131 of the Civil Code);
Turkey (Article 58 of the Code of Obligations); and.
Japan (see: Article 109 of the 1950 Mining Act, the 1972 Strict Liability for Pollution Damage Act, Article 25 of the 1968 Air Pollution Control Act and Article 19 of the 1970 Water Pollution Control Act).

The increasing acceptance of strict liability for ultrahazardous activities at the national level is evidence of an emerging principle of (national) law recognized by civilized nations. As known, according to Article 38(1)(c) of the Statute of the International Court of Justice, such a principle may also govern the relationship between sovereign States when there is no treaty or rule of customary international law calling for the application of a different principle or rule.

Paragraph 2 deals with the liability for activities which at the time that they were conducted were not known nor ought to have been known to be harmful, but appear later to have given rise to transboundary interferences causing substantial harm. Paragraph 2 provides that the State which undertook those activities itself or expressly or implicitly permitted such activities shall ensure that compensation is provided for the substantial extraterritorial harm caused by such activities.

Until the moment that the activities concerned became known or ought to have become known to cause substantial extraterritorial harm in the short or long run, the conducting or permission of such activities cannot be regarded unlawful, as there has not been question of a lack of due diligence or due care on the part of the State of origin (see the comment on Article 10).

The obligation laid down in Paragraph 2 constitutes again an instance of strict liability under international law to the extent that the State of origin is financially liable vis-à-vis the victim State.

The obligation laid down in Paragraph 2, however, may also be complied with by ensuring that private persons or entities which conducted the activity will be liable for the harmful consequences thereof vis-à-vis the victims.

Paragraph 2, which constitutes an instance of progressive development of international law, has to a large extent been inspired by the abominable Japanese Itai-Itai (cadmium poisoning) cases and Minamata (mercury poisoning) cases. Similar cases involving other substances may occur in the future and give rise to substantial extraterritorial harm.

The *rationale* for the strict liability provided for in Paragraph 2 is the same as for the strict liability envisaged in Paragraph 1. The financial burden for the substantial harm caused by certain not (yet) unlawful activities ought to be imposed on those who engage in those activities and receive the benefits of such activities. Moreover, the imposition of strict liability will no doubt greatly stimulate efforts designed to ensure that such activities will not cause substantial extraterritorial harm.

Article 12
Transboundary environmental interferences involving substantial harm far less than cost of prevention

1. If a State is planning to carry out or permit an activity which will entail a transboundary environmental interference causing harm which is substantial but far less than the overall technical and socio-economic cost or loss of benefits involved in preventing or reducing such interference, such State shall enter into negotiations with the affected State on the equitable conditions, both technical and financial, under which the activity could be carried out.

2. In the event of a failure to reach a solution on the basis of equitable principles within a period of 18 months after the beginning of the negotiations or within any other period of time agreed upon by

the States concerned, the dispute shall at the request of any of the
States concerned, and under the conditions set forth in Paragraphs 3
and 4 of Article 22, be submitted to conciliation or thereafter to
arbitration or judicial settlement in order to reach a solution on the
basis of equitable principles.

Comment

Article 12 deals with the case that a State is planning to carry out or permit
an activity which will entail a transboundary environmental interference
which causes harm which is substantial but far less than the overall technical
and socio-economic cost or loss of benefits involved in preventing or reducing
such interference. The activity envisaged here differs from those dealt with in
Paragraph 1 of Article 11 in that it concerns an activity of which it is
foreseeable what it will *definitely* cause substantial harm in an area under the
national jurisdiction of another State or in an area beyond the limits of
national jurisdiction, while the activities dealt with in Paragraph 1 of Article
11 "merely" involve a risk of causing extraterritorial harm of a possibly
exceptionally serious dimension, i.e. concern so-called ultrahazardous
activities.

The transboundary environmental interference envisaged in the present
article may be an instance of pollution involving substantial harm which can
only be avoided by the entire termination or forgoing of the, in itself, highly
beneficial activity, which gives rise to the interference. However, it also may
involve the building of a dam by a downstream State over a successive
international river giving rise to flooding of a certain part of the territory of
the upstream State thereby causing substantial harm.

As noted, the type of risk involving activities dealt with in Paragraph 1 of
Article 11 may be regarded lawful provided all possible precautionary
measures have been taken in order to minimize the risk. As we have also
seen, the State who carries out or permits the ultrahazardous activities must
ensure that compensation is provided should substantial extraterritorial harm
occur. This is, in fact, nothing else than the fair and equitable price which
ought to be paid for the lawful continuation of an ultrahazardous activity
which, on balance, must still be regarded as predominantly beneficial. It may
be wondered whether the same principle should not apply to the type of
activity envisaged in the present article, i.e. that it could invariably be
lawfully undertaken provided payment of compensation is ensured.

Little support can be found for this in the international practice of States,
possibly because situations calling for the application of that principle have so

far occurred only rarely. Convincing support for the application of the principle in such situations, however, can be found in national legal orders, where the principle appears to find general application in disputes between neighbouring landowners, so that it may be regarded as a general principle of national law recognized by civilized nations (in the sense of Article 38(1)(c) of the Statute of the International Court of Justice) which could be applied to interstate relationships (see: Lammers *op. cit.* in the comment on Article 9, at pp. 65 no. 1, 66, 118–119). The principle has further been adopted in certain international agreements dealing with the rights and duties of individuals on both sides of an international border in respect of, inter alia, transboundary water pollution (see: Lammers *op. cit.* at pp. 494–495, 499–500). Clear support for the principle can, moreover, be found in the award of the Trail Smelter Arbitration (see *ibid.* at pp. 524–525).

However, the application of the principle of strict liability—and the idea of balancing of interests which it implies—to activities *definitely* causing substantial extraterritorial harm, is generally regarded as considerably more revolutionary than the application of that principle to activities which "merely" involve a significant risk of harm as envisaged in Paragraph 1 of Article 11.

Hence, the present Article does not go that far. Instead it provides that the State planning to carry out or permit the activity concerned shall enter into negotiations with the affected State on the equitable conditions, both technical and financial, under which the activity could be carried out. Article 12, in fact, exempts the activity dealt with in that article from the operation of Article 10, which would otherwise apply to it. Thus, in spite of the fact that the activity would cause substantial extraterritorial harm, it is not regarded either as clearly unlawful, or as clearly lawful. Instead a duty to negotiate on the equitable conditions under which the activity could take place has been provided for.

Article 12 implies that, if the activity concerned is in fact to be carried out, the State who carries out or permits the activity must ensure that compensation—financial or in kind—is provided for as indemnification for the substantial harm caused. While in the case of Article 9—which deals with the equitable and reasonable use and apportionment of a transboundary natural resource or interferences therewith which do not constitute environmental interferences (see for these concepts *supra* the section on the use of terms)—the infliction of substantial harm (e.g. caused by diversion of water from an international watercourse) does not invariably involve a duty to provide for compensation, such compensation must be always provided for if the activity envisaged in the present article is to be carried out or permitted.

In the event of a failure to reach a solution on the basis of equitable principles within a period of 18 months after the beginning of the negotiations or within any other period of time agreed upon by the States concerned, the dispute shall at the request of any of the States concerned be submitted to conciliation for a recommended solution and, if necessary, eventually to arbitration or judicial settlement in order to reach a *binding* decision on the basis of equitable principles.

It may be argued that in certain cases a period of 18 months would not suffice to reach a solution on the basis of equitable principles. In reply to this, it can be said that a certain time limit is required in order to bring some structure to the process of arriving at an acceptable solution. Moreover, the parties themselves may extend the period beyond the 18 months limit, if they *both* so wish. Furthermore, even if a solution is not reached within 18 months or any other period of time, the next step will be a resort to a method of peaceful settlement of disputes—i.e. conciliation, or eventually even arbitration or judicial settlement—for which no strict time limits have been set.

Article 13
Non-discrimination between domestic and transboundary environmental interferences

Without prejudice to the principles laid down in Articles 10, 11 and 12 when calling for a more stringent approach, States shall, when considering under their domestic policy or law the permissibility of an environmental interference or a significant risk thereof, take into account the detrimental effects which are or may be caused by the environmental interference without discrimination as to whether the effects would occur inside or outside the area under their national jurisdiction.

Comment

According to this principle States are obliged vis-à-vis other States, when considering under their *domestic* policy or law the permissibility of environmental interferences or a significant risk thereof, to treat environmental interferences of which the detrimental effects are or may be mainly felt outside the area of their national jurisdiction in the same way as, or at least not less favourably than, those interferences of which the detrimental effects would be felt entirely inside the area under their national jurisdiction.

With the caveat to be noted below, this principle may be considered as an

emerging principle of international environmental law. It was adopted by the
Nordic States in Article 30 of the 1962 Treaty of Co-operation between
Denmark, Finland, Iceland, Norway and Sweden and later in Article 2 of the
1974 Nordic Environmental Protection Convention. The so-called non-
discrimination principle also has been increasingly recommended by certain
intergovernmental organizations or bodies.

The non-discrimination principle was adopted in the following:

1974 OECD Council Recommendation C(74)224 concerning Transfrontier
    Pollution (Annex Title C);
1977 OECD Council Recommendation C(77)28(Final) on Implementation of
    a Regime of Equal Right of Access and Non-Discrimination in relation to
    Transfrontier Pollution (Annex Title A(3));
1986 OECD Council Decision-Recommendation C(86)64(Final) on Exports
    of Hazardous Wastes from the OECD Area (as part of the binding decision
    of the OECD Council);
Principle 13 of the 1978 UNEP Draft Principles of Conduct on Shared
    Natural Resources; and
Conclusion 19(1) of the 1981 UNEP Conclusions of the Study on the Legal
    Aspects concerning the Environment related to Offshore Mining and
    Drilling within the Limits of National Jurisdiction.

The formulation of the principle formulated above has in fact been largely
inspired by UNEP Draft Principle of Conduct 13.

UNEP Draft Principle of Conduct 13 emphasizes that States should not
discriminate between environmental interferences which (may) cause detrimental effects within the jurisdiction of a State of origin and those of which
the detrimental effects are mainly felt outside the jurisdiction of the State of
origin when considering the permissibility of those interferences *under their
domestic environmental policy*. A duty not to discriminate between the two types
of interferences within the context of the application of a State's domestic
environmental policy does not appear to imply that principles of international environmental law which call for a more stringent approach to existing
or future transboundary environmental interferences than is required under
the non-discriminatory application of the domestic environmental policy or
law of the State of origin, are to be set aside.

This is made clear in the principle formulated above by the introductory
phrase: "Without prejudice to the principles laid down in Articles 10, 11
and 12 when calling for a more stringent approach . . .".

This also seems to be in line with the introductory phrase of Paragraph 4 of
Title C of the above-mentioned 1974 OECD Council Recommendation
C(74)224 which provides that: "Countries should *initially* base their action

on the principle of non-discrimination . . ." (emphasis added), and in line with Paragraphs 1 and 3 of Title A of the above-mentioned 1977 OECD Council Recommendation C(77)28(Final) which provides that the implementation of the environmental policy by States of origin should remain "consistent with their obligations and rights as regards the protection of the environment". Indeed the principle of non-discrimination was intended to provide a *minimum* level of protection below which OECD Member States were not supposed to come. This is not surprising for the effect of the principle of non-discrimination will, of course, depend on the stringency of the (applied) environmental policy and law of the State of origin. This level may be above or below the level which is required by the principles of environmental law laid down in Articles 10, 11 and 12 of the present text.

The introductory phrase to the principle formulated above ensures that the application of the non-discrimination principle by States "when considering under their domestic policy or law the permissibility of an environmental interference" will be without prejudice to the application of the principles of international environmental law contained in Articles 10, 11 and 12 of the present text when these call for a more stringent approach than is required under the domestic policy or law of the State of origin.

Article 14
General obligation to co-operate on transboundary environmental problems

1. States shall co-operate in good faith with the other States concerned in maintaining or attaining for each of them a reasonable and equitable use of a transboundary natural resource or in preventing or abating a transboundary environmental interference or significant risk thereof.
2. The co-operation shall, as much as possible, be aimed at arriving at an optimal use of the transboundary natural resource or at maximizing the effectiveness of measures to prevent or abate a transboundary environmental interference.

Comment

A proper implementation of the substantive rights and duties of States regarding the use of transboundary natural resources or the prevention or abatement of transboundary environmental interferences or significant risks thereof requires co-operation to that effect between the States concerned.

An important objective of this co-operation is, e.g. the collection and exchange of data concerning transboundary natural resources, including (transboundary interferences with) the uses made of such resources, or concerning transboundary environmental interferences. Another very important objective is usually to arrive at a more concrete delimitation of the substantive rights and duties of each State concerned within the context of a concrete situation allowing the States concerned to take the special features of that situation into account. This is especially true for the inherently flexible principle of equitable utilization of a transboundary national resource, the implementation of which involves, as we have seen, the taking into account of a great number of interrelated factors.

It also should be borne in mind that co-operation between the States concerned may not only serve to provide the conditions in which States will be able to *prevent* disputes arising from the use of a transboundary natural resource or from a transboundary environmental interference, but also to *solve* such disputes once they have arisen.

An essential condition for the process of co-operation is that it is pursued in good faith by the States concerned, each State having due regard for the other State's rights and interests.

Support for the existence of a general duty of States to also co-operate in good faith in order to maintain or restore a reasonable and equitable use of transboundary natural resources and/or to prevent or abate transboundary environmental interferences, is to be found in the first place in numerous international agreements which require such co-operation.

By way of example reference can be made to the following:

1963 Niamey Act regarding Navigation and Economic Co-operation between the States of the Niger Basin (Articles 4 and 5);

1963 Berne Convention on the International Commission for the Protection of the Rhine Against Pollution (amended in 1976);

1964 Agreement concerning the Use of Water Resources in Frontier Waters concluded between Poland and the USSR;

1968 Agreement concerning Co-operation in the Use of the Waters of Rivers Flowing through the Territory of Both Countries concluded between Bulgaria and Turkey;

1968 African Convention on the Conservation of Nature and Natural Resources (Article 16);

1971 Act of Santiago concerning Hydrologic Basins adopted between Argentina and Chile (Articles 3−8);

1974 Agreement concerning Water Economy Questions in Frontier Waters concluded between the German Democratic Republic and Czechoslovakia;

1974 Paris Convention for the Prevention of Pollution from Land-Based Sources;

1974 Helsinki Convention for the Baltic Sea Area;

1976 Barcelona Convention for the Mediterranean Sea and the 1980 Athens Protocol to that convention;

1978 Great Lakes Water Quality Agreement between Canada and the United States (Articles 7 – 10);

1979 ECE Convention on Long-Range Transboundary Air Pollution;

1980 Memorandum of Intent on Transboundary Air Pollution between Canada and the United States;

1982 UN Law of the Sea Convention (Articles 63, 66 – 67);

1983 Agreement on Co-operation for the Protection and Improvement of the Environment in the Border Area concluded between Mexico and the United States; and

1985 ASEAN Agreement on the Conservation of Nature and Natural Resources (Articles 19 en 20).

Support for the duty of States to co-operate in maintaining or restoring a reasonable and equitable use of transboundary natural resources or in counteracting transboundary environmental interferences is also to be found in various resolutions adopted by international organizations or by States at international conferences. See for example:

Principle 24 of the 1972 UN Declaration on the Human Environment;

Recommendations 51 and 72 adopted at the 1972 UN Conference on the Human Environment;

UNGA Resolution No. 2995 of 15 December 1972 on Co-operation between States in the Field of Environment (". . . in exercising their sovereignty over natural resources, States must seek, through effective bilateral and multilateral co-operation or through regional machinery, to preserve and improve the environment");

UNGA Resolution No. 3129 of 13 December 1973 on Co-operation in the Field of Environment concerning Natural Resources Shared by Two or More States;

1974 OECD Council Recommendation C(74)224 concerning Transfrontier Pollution;

Chapter 5 on Environment of the Final Act of the Conference on Security and Co-operation in Europe;

Recommendation 90 of the Action Plan adopted by the 1977 UN Mar del
Plata Water Conference; and
1978 UNEP Draft Principles of Conduct on Shared Natural Resources.

Finally, the Arbitral Tribunal in the *Lake Lanoux Case* (*Spain* v. *France*)
(in: 12 UN Rec. Int. Arb. Awards pp. 285–317, or in English in: 24 Int.
Law Rep. 1957 pp. 105–142) recognized the duty of the States to co-operate
in the use of the waters of an international watercourse in the following
terms:

"In fact, States are today perfectly conscious of the importance of the
conflicting interests brought into play by the industrial use of international rivers, and of the necessity to reconcile them by mutual concessions.
The only way to arrive at such compromises of interests is to conclude
agreements on an increasingly comprehensive basis. *International practice
reflects the conviction that States ought to strive to conclude such agreements; there
would thus appear to be an obligation to accept in good faith all communications
and contacts which could, by a broad confrontation of interests and by reciprocal
good will, provide States with the best conditions for concluding agreements . . .*"
(emphasis added).

As indicated in Paragraph 2 above the co-operation shall be aimed as much as
possible at reaching an optimal use of a transboundary natural resource or at
maximizing the effectiveness of measures to prevent or abate transfrontier
environmental interferences. In other words, co-operation should, where
possible, go beyond merely accommodating (possibly) conflicting uses of a
transboundary natural resource or co-ordinating efforts to prevent or abate
transboundary environmental interferences.

While the desirability of this approach is self-evident, it should at the
same time be borne in mind that an optimal use of a given natural resource
which would be possible in a politically undivided area can not always be
realized in a politically divided area without infringing upon the basic
principle of maintaining or attaining a reasonable and equitable delimitation
of the uses to be made by the various States concerned of a transboundary
natural resource. However, in other cases the goal of arriving at an optimal
use of a transboundary natural resource may well be compatible with that
principle.

The goal was, e.g. clearly pursued in the 1961 Treaty relating to
Co-operative Development of the Watercourses of the Columbia River
concluded between Canada and the United States. The treaty was based on

the principle that joint development of the Columbia river basin without regard to political frontiers resulted in greater advantage to both riparian States than individual alternatives available to each of them. Of interest also is the 1965 Agreement between the Netherlands and the United Kingdom relating to the Exploitation of Single Geological Structures Extending Across the Dividing Line on the Continental Shelf under the North Sea. According to Article 1, the Contracting Parties will seek to reach agreement as to the manner in which single geological mineral oil or gas structures or fields extending across the dividing line on the continental shelf "shall be *most effectively* exploited . . ." (emphasis added).

In support of the idea that States must as much as possible arrive at an optimal use of a transboundary natural resource reference may also be made to the 1954 Recommendation No. 4 submitted to governments by the ECE Committee on Electric Power with a view to promoting the hydroelectric development of successive rivers in Europe, in which States were recommended to reach agreements which "will ensure the most economic development of the river system". Reference must also be made to Article 3 of the Charter of Economic Rights and Duties of States proclaimed in UNGA Resolution No. 3281 of 12 December 1974 which has been quoted *infra* (see comment on Article 15).

As has been noted, co-operation between the States concerned should also, as much as possible, be aimed at maximizing the effectiveness of measures to prevent or abate transboundary environmental interferences. In certain cases this may, e.g. imply that one of two or more States which contribute to a transboundary environmental interference may be expected to prevent the discharge of a greater quantity of a certain pollutant than it would have been obliged to do at first sight, taking into account the quantities of that pollutant discharged by the other contributory States. This may explain why the main thrust of the efforts to decrease the salinity of the Rhine has been directed at reducing the discharges of waste salts into the Rhine by the French potassium mines, although Germany is also, if not a greater, contributor than France to the high salt content of the Rhine water. The reason is that the reduction of the salinity of the Rhine water can be realized with so much more effectiveness by the French potassium mines.

Article 15
Exchange of information

States shall provide the other States concerned upon their request and in a timely manner with all relevant and reasonably available data concerning a transboundary natural resource, including the uses made of such a resource and transboundary interferences with them, or concerning a transboundary environmental interference..

Comment

This article contains the basic obligation of States to provide the other States concerned upon their request and in a timely manner with relevant and reasonably available information concerning transboundary natural resources, including the uses or interferences with the uses made of such resources, or concerning transboundary environmental interferences. It involves, inter alia, a duty to provide the other States concerned with relevant and reasonably available information on the nature and extent of, or harm caused by, *specific* transboundary interferences *which have actually arisen*, so that the States concerned will be able to deal with those interferences on a sound data basis either through co-operation or some form of settlement of disputes. However, the article also purports to meet the need of States for a more general exchange of information on a regular basis concerning transboundary natural resources or the uses made thereof in order to allow the States concerned to continually analyze the conditions of the natural resource and make plans for a rational use of the natural resource. So, the duty to provide information may in principle pertain to many of the factors referred to in the comment on Article 9, which may have to be taken into account in order to arrive at a reasonable and equitable use of a transboundary natural resource.

Certain highly important forms of provision of information are not covered by the present article, but separately dealt with in other articles, viz. concerning the provision of information regarding planned activities which may entail a (significant risk of a) transboundary interference with the natural resources or the environment in another State (see Article 16) or the warning of other States in emergency situations (see Article 19).

The principle contained in the article above may be regarded as an established principle of international environmental law.

Thus, many treaties concerning the development, use or protection of international watercourses contain provisions with respect to information or data sharing. Reference may, inter alia, be made to the 1960 Indus Waters

Treaty between India and Pakistan, which provides for a regular exchange of various specified data regarding the flow and utilization of the Indus waters (Article 6). Similar provisions are to be found in the:

1954 Convention concerning Water Economy Questions relating to the Drava concluded between Austria and Yugoslavia (Article 1 of Annex B concerning the establishment of the Permanent Austro-Yugoslav Commission for the Drava);

1971 Declaration of Asunción on the Use of International Rivers adopted by the Ministers for Foreign Affairs of the countries of the La Plata River Basin (Argentina, Bolivia, Brazil, Paraguay and Uruguay) (Articles 3, 4);

1971 Act of Santiago concerning Hydrologic Basins adopted by Argentina and Chile (Article 8); or

1974 Agreement concerning Water Economy Questions in Frontier Rivers concluded between the German Democratic Republic and Czechoslovakia (Article 9).

An example of a provision specifically concerning water pollution is to be found in Article 9(3) of the 1978 Agreement on Great Lakes Water Quality concluded between Canada and the United States, which provides: "Each Party shall make available to the other at its request any data or other information in its control relating to water quality in the Great Lakes system."

Support for the principle contained in the present article is also to be found in treaty provisions concerning (long-distance) transboundary air pollution such as, for example, in Articles 3, 4, 8 and 9 of the 1979 ECE Convention on Long-Range Transboundary Air Pollution. Thus, Article 8, first sentence, and Paragraphs (a) and (f) of that convention provide:

"The Contracting Parties . . . shall, in their common interests, exchange available information on:
(a) data on emissions at periods of time to be agreed upon, of agreed air pollutants, starting with sulphur dioxide, coming from grid-units of agreed size; or on the fluxes of agreed air pollutants, starting with sulphur dioxide, across national borders, at distances and at periods of time to be agreed upon;

. . .

(f) physico-chemical and biological data relating to the effects of long-range transboundary air pollution and the extent of the damage which these data indicate can be attributed to long-range transboundary air pollution; . . ."

The reference in Paragraph (a) to elements which are subject to further agreement must be deemed to apply to the technical implementation and not to the obligation in principle to provide information on the subject-matter mentioned. Additional support for the principle contained in the present article can be found in Article 4 of the 1980 Memorandum of Intent on Transboundary Air Pollution between Canada and the United States and in Section 2 of the 1982 New York–Quebec Agreement on Acid Precipitation.

Other treaty provisions concerning exchange of data relate to marine pollution (whether caused by waterborne or airborne pollutants) such as, e.g. Article 10 of the 1978 Kuwait Regional Convention; Article 13 of the 1980 Athens Protocol to the 1976 Barcelona Convention for the Mediterranean Sea; Article 200 of the 1982 UN Law of the Sea Convention; or Article 13 of the 1983 Cartagena de Indias Convention for the Wider Caribbean Region.

A treaty obligation to exchange data to protect fauna and flora and to prevent and control diseases is to be found in the 1978 Brasilia Treaty for Amazonian Co-operation (Article 7; see also more generally, Article 15).

The principle contained in the article above has further been recommended in various resolutions adopted by international organs or organizations, viz. by the Governing Body of UNEP in Principles 5 and 7 of the 1978 UNEP Draft Principles of Conduct on Shared Natural Resources; by the Council of Ministers of the OECD in 1974 OECD Council Recommendation C(74)224 concerning Transfrontier Pollution (Annex Title G); and 1977 OECD Council Recommendation C(77)28(Final) concerning Implementation of a Regime of Equal Right of Access and Non-Discrimination in relation to Transfrontier Pollution (Annex Title C 8(a)). (See in this connection also the report by the OECD Environment Committee "Application of Information and Consultation Practices for Preventing Transfrontier Pollution", which was adopted by the Member States of OECD, in *Transfrontier Pollution and the Role of States*, OECD, Paris 1981, p. 8 et seq.) The UN General Assembly has on various occasions even expressed its support for the principle in mandatory terms. Thus UNGA Resolution No. 3129 of 13 December 1973 declared that "co-operation between countries sharing such natural resources and interested in their exploitation must be developed on the basis of a system of information and prior consultation". The General Assembly expressed the same view in Article 3 of the Charter of Economic Rights and Duties of States proclaimed in UNGA Resolution No. 3281 of 12 December 1974, which provides: "In the exploitation of natural resources shared by two or more countries, each State must co-operate on the basis of a system of information and prior consultations in order to achieve optimum use of such resources without causing damage to the legitimate interest of others".

The principle has finally been confirmed by the Institute of International Law in its 1979 Athens Resolution on Pollution of Rivers and Lakes and International Law (Article 7(a)), and by the International Law Association in its 1966 Helsinki Rules on the Uses of the Waters of International Rivers (Article 29), its 1980 Belgrade Articles on the Regulation of the Flow of Water of International Watercourses (Article 7(1)) and its 1982 Montreal Rules on Water Pollution in an International Drainage Basin (Article 5(a)).

It must be emphasized that the duty to provide information contained in the present article is limited to "all relevant and reasonably available data". This means that the State requesting the information must have an interest in receiving the information. This is to prevent States from being required to exert themselves and spend money in providing information which is not of real interest to the requesting State. In case the requested information is not reasonably available there is no duty either to provide such information (see, e.g. Article 3(b) of the 1971 Declaration of Asunción on the Use of International Rivers). Having regard to the general obligation to co-operate mentioned in Article 14 a State may, however, be expected to use its best efforts to provide such information if the State which requests the information is willing and able to pay the reasonable costs involved in obtaining that information (see, e.g. Article 7(1)(a) of the 1960 Indus Waters Treaty).

Article 16
Prior notice of planned activities, environmental impact assessments

1. States planning to carry out or permit activities which may entail a transboundary interference or a significant risk thereof with the reasonable and equitable use of a transboundary natural resource or which may entail a transboundary environmental interference or a significant risk thereof causing substantial harm in an area under national jurisdiction of another State or in an area beyond the limits of national jurisdiction shall give timely notice to the States concerned. In particular, they shall on their own initiative or upon request of the other States concerned provide such relevant information as will permit those other States to make an assessment of the probable effects of the planned activities.

2. When a State has reasonable grounds for believing that planned activities may have the effects referred to in Paragraph 1, it shall make an assessment of those effects before carrying out or permitting the planned activities.

Comment

The principle formulated in Paragraph 1 may be considered as a generally recognized principle of international environmental law. It provides that States which plan to carry out or permit activities which *may* result in a transboundary interference with the reasonable and equitable use of a transboundary natural resource in another State or in an area beyond the limits of national jurisdiction or which *may* entail a substantial transboundary interference with the environment of another State or with the environment beyond the limits of national jurisdiction shall give timely notice of such planned activities to such other States concerned.

The basic idea underlying the principle is to prevent the commission of unlawful transboundary interferences and to prevent other States from being confronted with *faits accomplis*. The principle may, therefore, also be looked upon as an application of the principle of good faith in international relations.

To achieve this basic idea States considering potentially unlawful transboundary interferences shall also, on their own initiative or upon request of potential victim States, provide such relevant information as will permit those States to assess the probable effects of the planned activities.

The obligation to give prior notice of planned activities has been adopted in many treaties. It may in fact be deemed to be implied in those treaty provisions to be discussed later which oblige States to enter into consultations on their own initiative with other States when planning activities which may entail transboundary interferences with the use of natural resources or the environment of those other States.

The obligation to give prior notice of planned activities as such appears, inter alia, in many treaties concerning the use of international watercourses. A good example is to be found in the treaties concluded by the basin States of the Niger. According to Article 4 of the 1963 Niamey Act regarding Navigation and Economic Co-operation between the States of the Niger Basin:

"The riparian States undertake to establish close co-operation with regard to the study and the execution of any project likely to have an appreciable effect on certain features of the regime of the river, its tributaries and sub-tributaries, their conditions of navigability, agricultural and industrial exploitation, the sanitary conditions of their waters, and the biological characteristics of their fauna and flora."

This provision is supplemented by Article 12 of the 1964 Niamey Agreement concerning the River Niger Commission and the Navigation and Transport on the River Niger which provides:

"In order to achieve maximum co-operation in connection with the matters mentioned in Article 4 of the Act of Niamey, the riparian States undertake to inform the Commission . . . at the earliest stage, of all studies and works upon which they propose to embark. They undertake further to abstain from carrying out . . . any works likely to pollute the waters, or any modification likely to affect biological characteristics of its fauna and flora, without adequate notice to, and prior consultation with, the Commission."

Other examples in Latin American treaties or international agreements are to be found in the 1971 Act of Santiago between Argentina and Chile concerning Hydrologic Basins (Article 5) and in the 1971 Buenos Aires Declaration between Argentina and Uruguay on Water Resources (Article 3). Noteworthy is that in these Latin American agreements the duty to give prior notice has been explicitly mentioned with regard to so-called successive international watercourses and that the utilization of the waters of so-called contiguous international watercourses in these and other Latin American agreements has been made subject to consent of the other riparian States. This implies by necessity prior notice to the other riparian States of a planned use which may substantially affect the use of the contiguous watercourse by those other States (see, e.g. the 1971 Declaration of Asunción on the Use of International Rivers (Article 1) and the above-mentioned 1971 Act of Santiago (Article 3)).

Examples of treaties in the Asian region requiring prior notice are the 1960 Indus Waters Treaty (Article 7(2)) and the 1985 ASEAN Agreement on the Conservation of Nature and Natural Resources (Articles 19(2)(d) and 20(3)(b)).

Examples of such provisions in Europe are to be found in the following: 1955 Agreement between Rumania and Yugoslavia on Questions of Water Control, Water Control Systems and Frontier Waters (Article 2); 1964 Agreement between Poland and the USSR concerning the Use of Water Resources in Frontier Waters (Article 6); 1974 Agreement between Czechoslovakia and the German Democratic Republic on Water Economy Questions in Frontier Waters (Article 1); and 1960 Frontier Treaty between the Federal Republic of Germany and the Netherlands (Article 60(1)). Provisions especially relating to water pollution are to be found in:

1960 Steckborn Convention on the Protection of Lake Constance against Pollution (Article 1);

1964 Agreement between Finland and the USSR concerning Frontier Water-courses (Article 4(3));

1974 Nordic Environmental Protection Convention; and

1980 Agreement between Norway and Finland concerning a Norwegian—Finnish Commission for Frontier Watercourses (Article 1).

In respect of North America reference may be made to the 1909 Boundary Waters Treaty between Canada and the United States (Articles 3 and 4) where the requirement of prior notice is implied in the requirement of approval by the International Joint Commission United States—Canada for uses and works which materially affect the level and flow of boundary waters in the territory of the other party.

Treaty provisions requiring prior notice may also be found for planned activities (possibly) entailing transfrontier radioactive contamination, viz., the 1966 Agreement between France and Belgium on Radiologic Protection concerning the Installations of the Nuclear Power Station of the Ardennes (Article 2); and 1977 Agreement between Denmark and Germany relating to Exchange of Information on Construction of Nuclear Installations along the Border.

A duty to give prior notice in the case of weather modification is to be found in the 1975 Agreement between Canada and the United States on the Exchange of Information on Weather Modification Activities (Article 2).

Examples relating to long-distance air pollution are to be found in the 1979 ECE Convention on Long-Range Transboundary Air Pollution (Article 8(b)) and the 1980 Memorandum of Intent between Canada and the United States concerning Transboundary Air Pollution. Finally mention may be made of the 1974 Nordic Environmental Protection Convention which contains an obligation to give prior notice applying generally to transboundary environmentally harmful activities (Article 5).

Information on planned activities which may cause transboundary environmental interferences is also usually given in the absence of existing treaty obligations to that effect. See, e.g. the various examples of State practice summarized by Rauschning in his Report on the ILA Draft Rules of International Law Applicable to Transfrontier Pollution (in: International

Law Association, Report of the 60th Conference, Montreal, 1982, pp. 172–173).

Broad support for the duty to give prior notice is further to be found in many resolutions adopted by intergovernmental organizations. Recommendation 51 adopted at the 1972 UN Conference on the Human Environment provided in Paragraph b(1) that ". . . when major water resource activities are contemplated that may have a significant environmental effect on another country, the other country should be notified in advance of the activity envisaged". Particularly relevant are also UNGA Resolutions Nos. 2995, 3129 and 3281 (Article 3) which state the duty to give prior notice in mandatory terms.

The duty to give prior notice is also recognized in Principles 6 and 7 of the 1978 UNEP Draft Principles of Conduct on Shared Natural Resources; Conclusion 17 of the 1981 UNEP Conclusions of the Study on the Legal Aspects concerning the Environment related to Offshore Mining and Drilling within the Limits of National jurisdiction; and in a number of OECD Council of Ministers recommendations, viz., 1974 OECD Council Recommendation C(74)224 concerning Transfrontier Pollution (Annex Title E); and 1977 OECD Council Recommendation C(77)28(Final) concerning Implementation of a Regime of Equal Right of Access and Non-Discrimination in relation to Transfrontier Pollution (Annex Title C 8(a)). (See in this connection also the report by the OECD Environment Committee referred to in the comment on Article 15). According to the UNEP and OECD recommendations transmission of information and data prohibited by national legislation is not required, but Principle 6(2) of the 1978 UNEP Draft Principles of Conduct on Shared Natural Resources provides that even in that case "the State . . . withholding such information shall nevertheless, on the basis . . . of the principle of good faith and in the spirit of good neighbourliness, co-operate with the other interested . . . States with the aim of finding a satisfactory solution".

Support for the duty to give prior notice is also to be found in: the 1982 EEC Council Directive on Major Accident Hazards of Certain Industrial Activities (Article 8(2)); 1985 EEC Council Directive on the Assessment of the Effects of Certain Public and Private Projects on the Environment (Article 7; see on this directive also the comment on Article 5); and in various other resolutions adopted by regional intergovernmental organizations or commissions. The Committee of Ministers of the Council of Europe adopted the principle in Resolution (71)5 on Air Pollution in Frontier Areas. Moreover, the duty appeared already in the 1933 Montevideo Declaration concerning Industrial and Agricultural Use of International Rivers which was approved by the Seventh International Conference of American States (Article 7). The notice was further to be ". . . accompanied by the necessary technical documentation in order that other interested States may judge the scope of such works . . .". Reference must also be made to Chapter E of the 1981 Conclusions reached by a UNEP working group with regard to Offshore Mining and Drilling (see the comment on Article 5).

The duty was further adopted in various draft agreements or propositions drawn up within the framework of regional intergovernmental organizations. It is found in a Draft Convention on the Industrial and Agricultural Use of International Rivers and Lakes prepared in 1965 by the Inter-American Judicial Committee of the Organization of American States (Article 8). A subcommittee of the Asian–African Legal Consultative Committee also implicity recognized the principle in the duty to enter into consultations in its Draft Propositions on the Law of International Rivers formulated in 1973 (Proposition 10).

Finally, it should be noted that the duty to give prior notice has been frequently adopted in resolutions of the Institute of International Law or the International Law Association, viz.:

1961 IIL Salzburg Resolution on the Use of International Non-Maritime Waters (Article 5);

1979 IIL Athens Resolution on Pollution of Rivers and Lakes and International Law (Article 7(1)(d));

1966 ILA Helsinki Rules on the Uses of the Waters of International Rivers (Article 29);

1980 ILA Belgrade Articles on the Regulation of the Flow of Water of International Watercourses (Article 7(1));

1982 ILA Montreal Rules on Water Pollution in an International Drainage Basin (Article 5(b)); and

1982 ILA Montreal Rules of International Law Applicable to Transfrontier Pollution (Article 5(1)).

The duty provided for in Paragraph 2 of the principle formulated above is of vital importance for the implementation of the rule contained in Paragraph 1. It obliges States to assess the effects of planned activities in order to verify whether these activities may have the effects referred to in Paragraph 1. Apart from that the assessment of the (potential) effects may serve to establish whether such activities will or will not lead to a breach of the substantive obligations incumbent on States to prevent unlawful transboundary interferences with the natural resources or environment in another State.

As we have already seen (see the comment on Article 5), growing support for the duty provided for in Paragraph 2 is to be found, inter alia, in a number of recent treaties dealing with marine pollution. It is also to be found in: the 1983 Agreement concluded between Mexico and the United States on Co-operation for the Protection and Improvement of the Environment in the Border Area (Articles 6, 7); 1985 ASEAN Agreement on the Conservation of Nature and Natural Resources (Articles 19(2)(c) and 20(3)(a)); and 1983 Cartagena de Indias Convention for the Wider Caribbean Region (Article 12).

Further support for the principle in Paragraph 2 is to be found in the 1985 EEC Council Directive mentioned above (Article 7) and in various resolutions of intergovernmental bodies, viz., Principle 4 of the 1978 UNEP Draft Principles of Conduct on Shared Natural Resources and certain OECD recommendations already mentioned earlier (see the comment on Article 5).

The principle has, moreover, been adopted in the 1979 IIL Athens Resolution on Pollution of Rivers and Lakes and International Law (Article 7(b)) and the 1982 ILA Montreal Rules of International Law Applicable to Transfrontier Pollution (Article 5(2)).

Article 17
Consultations

Consultations shall be held in good faith, upon request, at an early stage between, on the one hand, States whose reasonable and equitable use of a transboundary natural resource is or may be affected by a transboundary interference or whose environmental interests are or may be affected by a transboundary environmental interference and, on the other hand, States in whose area under national jurisdiction or under whose jurisdiction such a transboundary interference originates or may originate in connection with activities carried on or contemplated therein or thereunder.

Comment

The preceding principles stipulate a duty to provide information to potential victim States in various situations. The present well-established principle of international environmental law obliges the State of origin of a (potential) transboundary interference to go beyond that and to enter into consultations in good faith, and hence over a reasonable period of time, with the (potential) victim States upon their request in order to discuss and examine the implications of proposed or existing activities and to try to avoid or reduce (potential) adverse effects on the natural resources or environment of other States or in areas beyond the limits of national jurisdiction.

The obligation to enter into consultations in this situation does not stand on itself, but is similar in nature to the obligation to negotiate which has been recognized by the International Court of Justice in other situations which concerned the delimitation of adjacent or opposite continental shelf areas or of fishing rights in areas where exclusive fishing rights do not exist. With regard to these situations the Court observed: ". . . this obligation [to negotiate] merely constitutes a special application of a principle which underlies all international relations, and which is moreover recognized in Article 33 of the Charter of the United Nations as one of the methods for peaceful settlement of international disputes" (see: *North Sea Continental Shelf Cases* [1969] ICJ Rep. para. 86; see also: *Fisheries Jurisdiction Case* (Merits) [1974] ICJ Rep. 32).

The obligation to enter into consultations in the case of conflicting uses of the waters of an international watercourse was also recognized by the Arbitral Tribunal in its 1957 Award in the *Lake Lanoux Case* between France and Spain (in: 12 UN Rec. Int. Arb. Awards pp. 285–317, or in English in: 24 Int. Law Rep. 1957 pp. 105–142). Particularly interesting are the following observations made by the Tribunal with regard to the manner in which the interests of the other riparian States are to be safeguarded during the consultation process:

"The . . . question is to determine the method by which these interests can be safeguarded. If that method necessarily involves meetings and discussions, it cannot be confined to purely formal requirements, such as taking note of complaints, protests or representations made by the downstream State. The Tribunal is of the opinion that, according to the rules of good faith, the upstream State is under the obligation to take into consideration the various interests involved, to seek to give them every satisfaction compatible with the pursuit of its own interests, and to show that in this regard it is genuinely concerned to reconcile the interests of the other riparian State with its own."

The Tribunal emphasized in this case, as did the International Court of Justice in the above-mentioned cases, that even though the obligation to consult did not imply an obligation to reach agreement, it did oblige the States to pursue the consultations as far as possible with a view to concluding an agreement.

Broad support for the principle is not only to be found in international judicial or arbitral decisions, but also in many treaties.

Reference may be made to the following:

1964 Niamey Agreement concerning the River Niger Commission and the Navigation and Transport on the River Niger (Article 12);

1954 Agreement between Austria and Yugoslavia on Water Economy Questions relating to the Drava (Article 4);

1964 Agreement between Poland and the USSR concerning the Use of Water Resources in Frontier Waters (Article 6); and

1981 Convention concluded between Hungary and the USSR concerning Water Economy Questions in Frontier Waters (Articles 3–5).

Other treaty provisions which concern pollution of international watercourses are to be found in the 1960 Steckborn Convention on the Protection of Lake Constance against Pollution (Article 1) and the 1978 Great Lakes Water Quality Agreement between Canada and the United States (Articles 6(1)(1) and 10(1)). Of more general scope are the 1968 African Convention on the Conservation of Nature and Natural Resources (Article 5(2) and 14(3)) and the 1985 ASEAN Agreement on the Conservation of Nature and Natural Resources (Articles 19(2)(e) and 20(3)(c)).

A consultation obligation has further been adopted in various treaties concerning marine pollution, viz. the 1974 Paris Convention for the Prevention of Pollution from Land-Based Sources (Article 9) and the 1980 Athens Protocol to the 1976 Barcelona Convention for the Mediterranean Sea (Article 12).

A consultation obligation has also been adopted by the United States and Canada in Article 3 of their 1980 Memorandum of Intent concerning Transboundary Air Pollution which provides, inter alia, that the two governments "shall continue and expand their long-standing practice of advance notification and consultation on proposed actions involving a significant risk or potential risk of causing or increasing transboundary air pollution".

Particularly relevant is that practically all States—whether States of origin or victim States—involved in (long-distance) transboundary air pollution have accepted the duty to consult in respect of actual and potential instances of such pollution in Article 5 of the 1979 ECE Convention on Long-Range Transboundary Air Pollution. Relevant in this connection also is the 1980 EEC Council Directive on Air Quality Limit Values and Guide Values for Sulphur Dioxide and Suspended Particulates (Article 11).

Other treaties contain an obligation to consult for transboundary pollution in general, such as the 1974 Nordic Environmental Protection Convention (Article 11), or for weather modification, such as the 1975 Agreement between Canada and the United States on the Exchange of Information on Weather Modification Activities (Article 5).

The need for consultations in the case of (possible) transboundary interferences with natural resources or the environment in other States has also been recognized in various resolutions of intergovernmental bodies. While it is true that in some resolutions, consultations were merely recommended (see, e.g. the 1974 OECD Council Recommendation C(74)224 concerning Transfrontier Pollution (Annex Title E) and the 1977 OECD Council Recommendation C(77)28(Final) concerning Implementation of a Regime of Equal Right of Access and Non-Discrimination in relation to Transfrontier Pollution (Annex Title C) (see in this connection also the report by the OECD Environment Committee referred to in the comment on Article 15)) and in other resolutions the more neutral term "it is necessary for every State" was used (see Principles 5, 6 and 7 of the 1978 UNEP Draft Principles of Conduct on Shared Natural Resources), consultations were clearly considered obligatory in various broadly accepted resolutions of the UN General Assembly, viz., UNGA Resolution No. 3129 of 13 December 1973 and UNGA Resolution No. 3281 of 12 December 1974 already quoted earlier (see the comment on Article 15).

The duty to enter into consultations has, moreover, been frequently recognized in resolutions of non-governmental international organizations. It is to be found in the:

1961 IIL Salzburg Resolution on the Use of International Non-Maritime Waters (Article 6);

1979 IIL Athens Resolution on Pollution of Rivers and Lakes and International Law (Article 7(d));

1980 ILA Belgrade Articles on the Regulation of the Flow of Water of International Watercourses (Article 8);

1982 ILA Montreal Rules on Water Pollution in an International Drainage Basin (Article 6); and

1982 ILA Montreal Rules of International Law Applicable to Transfrontier Pollution (Article 6).

Article 18
Co-operative arrangements for environmental
assessment and protection

In order to maintain or attain a reasonable and equitable use of a transboundary natural resource or to prevent or abate transboundary environmental interferences or significant risks thereof the States concerned shall, inter alia:

(a) establish co-ordinated or unified systems for the collection and dissemination of data relating to the transboundary natural resource or for regular observation of transboundary environmental interferences;

(b) co-ordinate and, where appropriate, jointly undertake scientific or technical studies to that effect;

(c) establish by common agreement specific environmental standards, in particular environmental quality standards and emission standards;

(d) jointly establish or resort to an institutional mechanism or other appropriate arrangement.

Comment

(a) As we have already set forth in the comment on Article 15 relating to exchange of information, States shall provide other States concerned, upon their request, with all relevant and reasonably available data concerning a transboundary natural resource, including the uses made of such a resource and transboundary interferences with them, or concerning a transboundary environmental interference. There is a growing awareness on the part of States that the regular collection of such data requires the setting up of systems, which in order that the collected data will be comparable and complementary should be co-ordinated or even unified systems. This is reflected in Paragraph (a) of the principle formulated above.

Such systems have, e.g. already been agreed upon in the 1944 Water Treaty concluded between the United States and Mexico where it has been provided in Article 24(f):

"The Commission [i.e. the International Boundary and Water Commission] shall construct, operate and maintain upon the limitrophe parts of the international streams, and each Section [i.e. the United States Section or the Mexican Section of the Commission] shall severally construct, operate and maintain upon the parts of the international streams and their tributaries within the boundaries of its own country, such stream gauging stations as may be needed to provide hydrographic data necessary or convenient for the proper functioning of this Treaty. The data so obtained shall be compiled and periodically exchanged between the two Sections."

Similar provisions have been agreed on in the 1957 Agreement between Greece and Yugoslavia on a Procedure and Plan for Co-operation in Making Hydroeconomic Studies of the Drainage Area of Lake Dojran (see esp. Section A Ch. II and Section B Ch. II); 1974 Agreement concluded between Czechoslovakia and the German Democratic Republic on Water Economy Questions in Frontier Waters (Article 9(1)); or 1985 ASEAN Agreement on the Conservation of Nature and Natural Resources (Article 18: "The Contracting Parties shall . . . endeavour . . . to collaborate in monitoring activities.").

Co-ordinated monitoring activities are particularly required in order to counteract transboundary pollution. Illustrative is Article 6(1)(m) of the 1978 Great Lakes Water Quality Agreement where Canada and the United States agreed that programmes and measures to be developed shall include:

"*Surveillance and Monitoring*. Implementation of a co-ordinated surveillance and monitoring programme in the Great Lakes System, in accordance with Annex II, to assess compliance with pollution control requirements and achievement of the objectives, to provide information for measuring local and whole lake response to control measures, and to identify emerging problems."

Other agreements contain provisions specifically relating to the monitoring of transboundary air pollution, e.g. the 1980 Memorandum of Intent on Transboundary Air Pollution concluded between Canada and the United States (Article 4) and the 1979 ECE Convention on Long-Range Transboundary Air Pollution, where the Contracting Parties agreed in Article 9 to implement and develop further the already existing "Co-operative programme for the monitoring and evaluation of long-range transmission of air pollutants in Europe" (EMEP).

Additional support for Paragraph (a) of the principle formulated above is to be found in Recommendation 79 (concerning air pollution) of the 1972 UN Conference on the Human Environment, Recommendation 86(f) of the 1977 UN Mar del Plata Water Conference and in the 1974 OECD Council Recommendation C(74)224 concerning Transfrontier Pollution (Annex Title G).

As far as non-intergovernmental international organizations are concerned reference ought to be made to the 1979 IIL Athens Resolution on Pollution of Rivers and Lakes and International Law (Article 7(h)), and the 1982 ILA Montreal Rules on Water Pollution in an International Drainage Basin (Article 7(b)).

(b) Co-ordinated and, where appropriate, even joint scientific or technical studies to be agreed on and undertaken by the States concerned may greatly contribute to a rational and equitable use of a transboundary natural resource. Such studies are to date also an indispensible means of co-operation for preventing or abating transboundary environmental interferences. A notable example of this generally recognized truth is to be found in Article 7 of the 1979 ECE Convention on Long-Range Transboundary Air Pollution, which provides:

"The Contracting Parties, as appropriate to their needs, shall initiate and co-operate in the conduct of research and/or development of:
(a) existing and proposed technologies for reducing emissions of sulphur compounds and other major air pollutants, including technical and economic feasibility, and environmental consequences;
(b) instrumentation and other techniques for monitoring and measuring emission rates and ambient concentrations of air pollutants;
(c) improved models for a better understanding of the transmission of long-range transboundary air pollutants;
(d) the effects of sulphur compounds and other major air pollutants on human health and the environment, including agriculture, forestry, materials, aquatic and other natural ecosystems and visibility, with a view to establishing a scientific basis for dose/effect relationships designed to protect the environment;
(e) the economic, social and environmental assessment of alternative measures for attaining environmental objectives including the reduction of long-range transboundary air pollution; . . ."

A relevant example relating to the use of the water of an international drainage basin is to be found in Article 5 of the 1963 Niamey Act regarding Navigation and Economic Co-operation between the States of the Niger Basin:

"In order to further their co-operation for the attainment of the objectives of this Act, the riparian States undertake to establish an Inter-Governmental Organization which will be entrusted with the task of encouraging, promoting and co-ordinating the studies and programmes concerning the exploitation of the resources of the River Niger basin. . . ."

Mention can also be made of the following:

1944 Agreement between Canada and the United States relating to a Study to be Made by the International Joint Commission with respect to the Upper Columbia River Basin (on navigation, power development, irrigation, flood control and other beneficial public uses and purposes);

1950 Agreement between the United Kingdom (on behalf of Uganda) and Egypt regarding Co-operation in Meteorological and Hydrological Surveys in Certain Areas of the Nile Basin;

1957 Agreement between Greece and Yugoslavia on a Procedure and Plan for Co-operation in Making Hydroeconomic Studies of the Drainage Area of Lake Dojran;

1958 Agreement between Argentina and Paraguay concerning a Study of the Utilization of the Water Power of the Apipe Falls;

1983 Agreement between Canada and the United States to Track Air Pollution across Eastern North America (Acid Rain Research); and

1985 ASEAN Agreement on the Conservation of Nature and Natural Resources (Articles 18(2)(f), and 19(2)(g)).

Co-ordinated or joint scientific and technical studies have also been repeatedly recommended by international organizations or conferences, e.g. in Recommendation 48 adopted by the 1972 UN Conference on the Human Environment; 1974 OECD Council Recommendation C(74)224 concerning Transfrontier Pollution (Annex Title G 12); Principle 8 of the 1978 UNEP Draft Principles of Conduct on Shared Natural Resources.

Co-ordinated or joint studies, especially to combat pollution of the waters of an international drainage basin, are further recommended in the 1979 IIL Athens Resolution on Pollution of Rivers and Lakes and International Law (Article 8(e)) and in the 1982 ILA Montreal Rules on Water Pollution in an International Drainage Basin (Article 7(a)).

(c) While, as we have seen, general international law imposes certain obligations of a rather general and vague nature upon States to prevent or abate substantial interferences with the reasonable and equitable use of a transboundary natural resource or to prevent or abate substantial transboundary environmental interferences, such obligations must usually be given a more specific content, which takes into account the nature of the interests to be protected as well as the nature of the (potential) interference with those interests. Such norms are in fact an important legal tool to make international environmental law effective. Hence Paragraph (c) of the principle formulated above provides that States must establish, by common agreement, specific environmental standards in various forms, such as environmental quality standards or emission standards (see on the nature of these standards: the comment on Article 4).

Environmental quality standards specifically concerning pollution of international watercourses are, inter alia, to be found in Annex III to the 1960 Treaty between Belgium and the Netherlands concerning the Improvement of the Terneuzen and Ghent Canal. A specific standard on the salinity of the Colorado river waters flowing from the United States into Mexico has been adopted in the 1973 Agreement between Mexico and the United States concerning the Permanent and Definitive Solution to the International Problem of the Salinity of the Colorado River. Reference should also be made to Articles 1–4 and Annex I of the 1978 Agreement on Great Lakes Water Quality concluded between Canada and the United States. In 1982 the Commission for the Protection of the Rhine against Pollution recommended a certain water quality objective for chromium for adoption in the national programmes of the Member States to be drawn up by those States in accordance with the 1976 Bonn Convention on the Protection of the Rhine against Chemical Pollution (Article 6).

The adoption of environmental quality standards in general was recommended in the 1974 OECD Council Recommendation C(74)224 concerning Transfrontier Pollution (Annex Title B 1(b)), while water quality standards and/or emission standards for particular international water bodies have been recommended in Principle 13 of the 1980 ECE Declaration of Policy on Prevention and Control of Water Pollution.

The establishment of emission standards has further been envisaged in the 1964 Agreement between Poland and the USSR concerning the Use of Water Resources in Frontier Waters (Article 16) and in the 1976 Bonn Convention on the Protection of the Rhine against Chemical Pollution (Article 2 et seq.). Such standards—called "limit values"—have now been agreed on by the Parties to the Bonn Convention in respect of mercury and cadmium. It should also be noted that prescriptions for maximum sulphur dioxide emissions for various seasons and under various wind conditions constituted an important element of the measures ordered by the Arbitral Tribunal in the *Trail Smelter Case* in order to reduce transboundary air pollution into the United States.

Support for the idea that States must establish by common agreement specific environmental standards, in particular quality norms for international watercourses is also to be found in the 1979 IIL Athens Resolution on

Pollution of Rivers and Lakes and International Law (Article 7(f)) and the 1982 ILA Montreal Rules on Water Pollution in an International Drainage Basin (Article 7(c)).

(d) Depending on the nature and extent of actual or potential transboundary interferences with the use of a natural resource or the environment in general, the establishment of some form of joint institutionalized mechanism or other appropriate arrangement between the States concerned may become useful or even indispensible. It will provide an opportunity for regular contacts between representatives of the States concerned with the basic objective of the promotion of the effective implementation of an applicable international agreement and/or of the principles contained in this paper. No particular form of institutional framework for co-operation is advocated. The States concerned may decide to jointly establish a new international body but also to resort for certain purposes to an already existing international institution. Moreover, the functions and powers of such an international body may vary greatly.

In the past, many new institutional mechanisms have been established in order to deal more or less generally with problems concerning the utilization of the waters of international watercourses. By way of example, mention may be made of the following:

International Joint Commission United States−Canada which was established under the 1909 Boundary Waters Treaty concluded between the United States and Great Britain on behalf of Canada (Article 7 et seq.);

International Boundary and Water Commission, United States and Mexico, established under the 1889 Boundary Convention and given additional powers in the 1944 Water Treaty concluded between Mexico and the United States;

Administrative Commission of the La Plata River established under the 1973 Treaty concluded between Argentina and Uruguay concerning the La Plata River and its Maritime Limits (Article 59 et seq.);

River Niger Commission established under the 1964 Niamey Agreement concerning the River Niger Commission and the Navigation and Transport on the River Niger;

Permanent Indus Commission established under the 1960 Indus Waters Treaty (Article 8);

Joint Finnish−Soviet Commission on the Utilization of Frontier Watercourses established under the 1964 Agreement concluded between Finland and the USSR concerning Frontier Watercourses (Article 6 et seq.);

Permanent Netherlands−German Boundary Waters Commission established under the 1960 Frontier Treaty concluded between the Federal Republic of Germany and the Netherlands (Article 64 et seq.); and

Frontier Water Commission established under the 1974 Agreement concluded between Czechoslovakia and the German Democratic Republic concerning Water Economy Questions in Frontier Waters (Article 13).

Reference should here also be made to Article 5(2) of the 1968 African Convention on the Conservation of Nature and Natural Resources which provides:

> "Where surface or underground water resources are shared by two or more of the Contracting States, the latter shall act in consultation, and if the need arises, set up inter-State Commissions to study and resolve problems arising from the joint use of these resources, and for the joint development and conservation thereof."

It also happens that new institutional mechanisms are established in order to deal only with one particular aspect of the use of international watercourses. Thus, various international commissions have been established which must cope with the problem of pollution of certain international rivers or lakes, such as the Rhine, the Moselle, the Sarre, Lake Constance, Lake Geneva, the Italian–Swiss frontier waters or the Belgian–French–Luxembourg frontier waters (see: Lammers, *op. cit. supra* in the comment on Article 9, at pp. 168–170, 213–214, 243–244).

As we have already seen (see the comment on Article 8) new international commissions or sometimes a whole new organization have been created for protection of marine waters, while in other cases conventions have provided for regular meetings of the Parties and designated UNEP as responsible for carrying out various secretarial functions.

Institutional mechanisms or other appropriate arrangements have also been created in order to cope with transboundary interferences other than those connected with the use or pollution of international watercourses or the marine environment.

Thus, some of the commissions already mentioned may deal, additionally, with transboundary air pollution problems or other types of transboundary environmental interferences, viz. the International Joint Commission United States–Canada and the International Boundary and Water Commission, United States and Mexico.

The 1979 ECE Convention on Long-Range Transboundary Air Pollution envisaged the establishment of a so-called Executive Body consisting of representatives of the Parties within the framework of the (already existing)

Committee of Senior Advisors to ECE Governments on Environmental Problems. It is the task of the Executive Body to review the implementation of the ECE Convention.

A rather recent development is the creation of institutional mechanisms for the exchange of information and for consultations concerning the establishment of nuclear power stations in border areas. Such power stations may not only lead to injurious changes in the temperature or the flow of the water of international watercourses, but also raise the important question of the safety of the stations and of the protection of the population and the environment against radioactive contamination. Co-operation in bi- or trilateral bodies has taken place in this field between, on the one hand, the Federal Republic of Germany, and on the other hand, Austria, Denmark, France, Luxembourg, the Netherlands and Switzerland (see for a survey of these bodies: Verhandlungen des Deutschen Bundestages, Stenographische Berichte, 8/16 Session of 3 March 1977, p. 892; also the 1977 Agreement between the Federal Republic of Germany and Denmark relating to Exchange of Information on the Construction of Nuclear Installations along the Border).

The need to institutionalize co-operation through appropriate mechanisms or arrangements in the field of shared natural resources or transboundary environmental interferences has also often been acknowledged in resolutions of intergovernmental organizations or conferences such as in:

Recommendation 51 adopted during the 1972 UN Conference on the Human Environment ("Governments [should] consider the creation of river-basin commissions or other appropriate machinery for co-operation between interested States for water resources common to more than one jurisdiction".);

Recommendations 85 and 86(b) of the 1977 UN Mar del Plata Water Conference (Recommendation 85: "Countries sharing water resources . . . should . . . co-operate in the establishment of . . . institutions necessary for the co-ordinated development of such resources . . ."; Recommendation 86(b) ". . . should establish joint committees . . .");

Principle 2 of the 1978 UNEP Draft Principles of Conduct on Shared Natural Resources (". . . institutional structures, such as joint international commissions, for consultations on environmental problems relating to the protection and use of shared natural resources"); and

the 1974 OECD Council Recommendation C(74)224 concerning Transfrontier Pollution (Annex Title H: "countries . . . should consider the advantages of co-operation, by setting up international commissions or other bodies, or by strengthening existing institutions . . .").

Finally, similar recommendations have also repeatedly been made by non-intergovernmental international organizations. For instance in the:

1911 IIL Madrid Resolution on International Regulations regarding the Use of International Watercourses for Purposes other than Navigation (Article 2(7));

1961 IIL Salzburg Resolution on the Use of International Non-Maritime Waters (Article 9);

1979 IIL Athens Resolution on Pollution of Rivers and Lakes and International Law (Article 7(g));

1976 ILA Madrid Resolution on International Water Resources Administration (with an Annex containing Guidelines for the Establishment of an International Water Resources Administration); and

1982 ILA Montreal Rules on Water Pollution in an International Drainage Basin (Article 7).

Article 19
Emergency situations

1. In the case of an emergency situation or other change of circumstances suddenly giving rise to a transboundary interference or a significant risk thereof with the reasonable and equitable use of a transboundary natural resource or to a transboundary environmental interference or a significant risk thereof, causing substantial harm in an area under national jurisdiction of another State or in an area beyond the limits of national jurisdiction, the State in whose area under national jurisdiction or under whose jurisdiction the interference originates shall promptly warn the other States concerned, provide them with such pertinent information as will enable them to minimize the transboundary environmental interference, inform them of steps taken to abate the cause of the transboundary environmental interference, and co-operate with those States in order to prevent or minimize the harmful effects of such an emergency situation or other change of circumstances.

2. States shall develop contingency plans in order to prevent or minimize the harmful effects of an emergency situation or other change of circumstances referred to in Paragraph 1.

Comment

According to this principle States are obliged to promptly warn a potential victim State and to provide that State with all pertinent information in the case of an emergency situation or other change of circumstances *suddenly* giving rise to an imminent transboundary interference with the natural resources or the environment of that State possibly causing substantial harm in that State. The principle further obliges the State to co-operate with the potential victim State in preventing or minimizing the harmful effects and in developing plans for that purpose.

In the *Corfu Channel Case* (Merits) ([1949] ICJ Rep. 22) the International Court of Justice mentioned "elementary considerations of humanity" as a basis for a duty of States to warn those who were exposed to situations of danger threatening human health or even life. These "elementary considerations of humanity" may also serve as a basis for a duty of States to warn other States in emergency situations covered by the present principle which involve a serious danger for human health or life.

Support for a duty to promptly warn potential victim States in an emergency situation or other change of circumstances suddenly giving rise to a (significant risk of a) transboundary interference causing substantial harm—albeit not necessarily in the form of an impairment of human health or even loss of life—and for the duty to co-operate with those States in order to prevent or minimize the harmful effects thereof is also to be found in many treaties.

Many of these treaties concern international watercourses. In some treaty provisions the duty to warn concerns only floods, floating ice or similar dangers, which may or may not be caused by human conduct such as, e.g. in:

1948 Agreement between Poland and the USSR concerning the Regime of the Soviet—Polish State Frontier (Article 19);

1955 Agreement between Rumania and Yugoslavia on Questions of Water Control, Water Control Systems and Frontier Waters (Article 13); and

1965 Agreement between the German Democratic Republic and Poland on Co-operation in Water Economy Questions in Frontier Waters (Article 9).

Examples of a duty to warn relating to pollution of an international watercourse are to be found in:

1976 Bonn Convention on the Protection of the Rhine against Chemical Pollution (Article 11);

1976 Bonn Convention on the Protection of the Rhine against Pollution by Chlorides (Article 11);

above-mentioned 1965 Agreement between the German Democratic
Republic and Poland (Article 8); and

1978 Great Lakes Water Quality Agreement between Canada and the United
States (Articles 6(1)(i) and 10).

The latter agreement also provides for the maintenance of a joint contingency
plan for use in the event of a discharge or the imminent threat of a discharge
of oil or hazardous polluting substances (Article 5(1)(i) and Annex 9).

Mention should also be made of the following:

1966 Agreement between Belgium and France on Radiologic Protection
concerning the Installations of the Nuclear Power Station of the Ardennes
(Articles 2, 4 and Annex III) which concerns incidents involving radioactive pollutants;

1973 Agreement between the Federal Republic of Germany and the German
Democratic Republic concerning the Prevention and Abatement of Injurious Incidences in the Frontier Area (Articles 2, 3 and 4) which relates to a
whole range of transboundary environmental interferences (i.e. floods,
floating ice, contagious diseases, injurious plants or animals, water and air
pollution, explosions, radiation, etc.);

1983 Agreement between Mexico and the United States on Co-operation in
the Solution of Environmental Problems in the Border Area (Article 1);
and

1985 ASEAN Agreement on the Conservation of Nature and Natural
Resources (Articles 19(2)(f) and 20(3)(d)).

There are also many treaties which provide for a duty to warn and to
co-operate in the case of emergency situations (probably) giving rise to
marine pollution, viz.:

1969 Bonn Agreement for Co-operation in Dealing with Water Pollution of
the North Sea by Oil (Articles 3, 5);

1973 London International Convention for the Prevention of Pollution from
Ships (Article 8);

1974 Helsinki Convention for the Protection of the Marine Environment
of the Baltic Sea Area (Article 11 and Annex 6, Reg. 5);

1974 Paris Convention for the Prevention of Marine Pollution from Land-
Based Sources (Article 13);

1976 Barcelona Convention for the Mediterranean Sea (Article 9) and the
related 1976 Barcelona Protocol concerning Co-operation in Cases of
Emergency;

1978 Kuwait Regional Convention (Article 9) and the related 1978 Kuwait
Protocol concerning Regional Co-operation in Cases of Emergency;

1981 Abidjan Convention for the West and Central African Region (Article 12);

1982 Jeddah Regional Convention (Article 9); and

1983 Cartagena de Indias Convention for the Wider Caribbean Region (Article 9);

Relevant also are certain provisions in the 1982 UN Law of the Sea Convention. Article 198 of this convention provides:

"When a State becomes aware of cases in which the marine environment is in imminent danger of being damaged by pollution, it shall immediately notify other States it deems likely to be affected by such damage, as well as the competent international organizations."

Article 199 dealing with contingency plans provides:

"In the cases referred to in Article 198, States . . . shall co-operate, to the extent possible, in eliminating the effects of pollution and preventing or minimizing the damage. To this end, States shall jointly develop and promote contingency plans for responding to pollution incidents in the marine environment."

Support for the duty to warn other potentially affected States and to co-operate with those States in preventing or minimizing suddenly arising transboundary harmful effects on the natural resources or the environment of those States in emergency situations is also to be found in Principle 9 of the 1978 UNEP Draft Principles of Conduct on Shared Natural Resources and in 1974 OECD Council Recommendation C(74)224 concerning Transfrontier Pollution (Annex Title F).

Support for the principle formulated above may finally also be found in resolutions of non-intergovernmental organizations, viz., in the 1979 IIL Athens Resolution on Pollution of Rivers and Lakes and International Law (Article 7(c)); 1982 ILA Montreal Rules of International Law Applicable to Transfrontier Pollution (Article 7); and 1982 ILA Montreal Rules on Water Pollution in an International Drainage Basin (Article 5(c)).

Article 20
Non-intergovernmental proceedings

States shall provide remedies for persons who have been or may be detrimentally affected by a transboundary interference with their use of a transboundary natural resource or by a transboundary environmental interference. In particular, States of origin shall grant those persons equal access as well as due process and equal treatment in the same administrative and judicial proceedings as are available to persons within their own jurisdiction who have been or may be similarly affected.

Comment

The principle contained in Article 13 merely prohibits States of origin of a transboundary environmental interference to discriminate between interferences of which the detrimental effects will be mainly felt outside the area under their jurisdiction on the one hand, and those of which the detrimental effects would be felt inside the area under their national jurisdiction on the other hand, without purporting to give any legal remedies to (potentially) affected foreign persons or non-State entities. In contradistinction, the principle formulated above stipulates that States must provide legal remedies for persons who have been or may be adversely affected by a transboundary interference with their use of a transboundary natural resource or by a transboundary environmental interference. The first sentence of the principle formulated above implies a duty for both the State of origin and the (possibly) affected State to provide, where necessary by agreement or otherwise, for such matters as the jurisdiction of courts, the applicable law and the enforcement of administrative and judicial decisions. The second sentence of the principle relates more particularly to the State of origin urging it to avoid discrimination by granting (potentially) affected foreign victims equivalent access to and treatment in the same administrative and judicial proceedings as are available to persons within their own jurisdiction who have been or may be similarly affected. In short, while the first sentence obliges both States of origin and (potentially) affected States to provide for legal remedies when these are not yet available, the second sentence obliges the State of origin not to discriminate between domestic victims and foreign victims in the application of remedies available to its own residents. Hereinafter, attention will first be given to non-intergovernmental proceedings in the State of origin. Thereafter, those in the (potentially) affected State will be discussed. These proceedings are all *domestic* and *national* proceedings. States, however, may also create *international* non-intergovernmental proceedings to which persons who (may) create a transboundary interference or (potentially) affected persons may have (to take) resort. Such proceedings which may also be covered by the notion of remedies in the first sentence of Principle 20 should also be briefly discussed.

Proceedings in the State of origin

There are various reasons why (potentially) affected foreign persons should be given access to, and adequate treatment by, the administrative and judicial authorities in the State of origin of a transboundary interference.

It allows the (potential) victims to take action *proprio motu* for the protection of their interests instead of waiting until action is taken by their government. This government may not be willing to hold the State of origin responsible, e.g. out of fear of being itself confronted with counterclaims by the other State concerning transboundary interferences which it may in its turn cause in the area of national jurisdiction of the other State or simply because it does not wish to burden the perhaps already delicate relation with the State of origin. It may also be that the (potentially) affected State may not be successful for various reasons in having the interference abolished or reduced at the interstate level, e.g. because the State of origin cannot be deemed to have breached an international duty of due diligence to prevent transboundary pollution. From the viewpoint of the State of origin domestic proceedings may well be preferred as such proceedings may prevent the State of origin from being held responsible at the intergovernmental level by the (potentially) affected State.

However, while there are good reasons why in certain cases resort to domestic proceedings in the State of origin is to be preferred over the intergovernmental approach, such proceedings will not always be possible.

In some countries (potentially) affected foreign persons will have *locus standi* before administrative authorities or courts, e.g. in France (see: the decision rendered by the Judicial Division of the *Conseil d'Etat* on 23 December 1981 concerning objections raised, inter alia, by certain German and Luxembourg municipalities, nature conservation associations and citizens against the Decree of 11 October 1978 recognizing the public utility of the nuclear power station at Cattenom (France), in Rev. Jur. de l'Environnement 1982 p. 295; see also: the decision of 27 July 1983 of the *Tribunal Administratif* of Strasbourg concerning a request of French potassium mines for a licence to continue to discharge waste salts into the Rhine, in *La Province de la Hollande septentrionale et autres* v. *Etat-Ministre de l'Environnement (Commissaire de la République du Haut-Rhin)* TA 227/81, 700/81 to 232/81, and 1197/81 and the decision rendered by the Judicial Division of the Conseil d'Etat on 18 April 1986, in *Société les Mines de Potasse d'Alsace* v. *La Province de la Hollande septentrionale et autres*, Case No. 53/934), or in the Netherlands (see: the decision of 3 October 1978 of the Chairman of the Judicial Division of the Dutch Council of State concerning objections raised by the German town of Borkum against a licence issued by the Dutch Ministry of Transport and Water Management provisionally allowing certain waste water discharges in the Ems-Dollard estuary, in Administratieve Beslissingen 1979 p. 353), or in Switzerland (see: the decision of the Swiss *Bundesrat* of 22 August 1979 explicitly recognizing the right of certain private persons living in Germany to lodge an administrative appeal against the licences for the construction of a nuclear power station in Leibstadt, in 44 Verwaltungspraxis der Bundesbehörden 1980 p. 86).

In other countries the administrative authorities and/or courts take the view that the scope of the applicable administrative law is strictly territorial, so that foreign interests are not considered to be legally affected nor protected by that law with the consequence that the foreign complainants are denied *locus standi*. This is the case in Austria (see, e.g. the 1913 decision of the Austrian Imperial and Royal Administrative Court concerning the diversion of water from the Leithe River, in 7 AJIL 1913 pp. 653–665, or the decision of 30 May 1969 of the Austrian Administrative Court in the *Salzburg Airport case* in Erkentnisse und Beschlüsse des Verwaltungsgerichtshofs No. 7582(A) p. 264 (1964)), or in the Federal Republic of Germany (see the 1985 decision of the *Verwaltungsgericht* Oldenburg, 3rd Chamber Osnabrück in *Hamers* v. *den Niedersächsischen Minister für Bundesangelegenheiten* (Case 3 OS VG A 259/82/Mi)).

In some States of origin civil proceedings may be brought only before the courts of the place of the injury (see, e.g. English, Canadian and other Commonwealth case law concerning injury to foreign real property in the House of Lords decision *British South Africa Company* v. *Companhia de Moçambique* [1983] AC 602; or Article 20 of the Italian Code of Civil Procedure).

While in the case of proceedings before administrative authorities or courts the administrative policy or law of the State of origin will be determinative, in civil proceedings problems concerning the choice of the applicable law may rise.

Questions concerning the competence of, or the policy or law to be applied by, the administrative or judicial (whether administrative, civil or criminal) authorities of the State of origin have to some extent become the subject of treaties or recommendations by intergovernmental organizations.

Thus the 1968 European Community Convention on Jurisdiction and Enforcement of Judgments in Civil and Commercial Matters (hereafter: 1968 EC Jurisdiction and Enforcement of Judgments Convention) allows, in the interpretation given by the court of Justice of the European Community to Article 5(3) of that Convention, civil torts to be brought before the courts of

the State of origin or before those of the affected State (see Judgment of 30 November 1976, in *Report of Cases before the Court* 1976–8 (Case 21/76)).
Reference must also be made to the following:

1909 Boundary Waters Treaty between Canada and the United States (Article 2);

1974 Nordic Environmental Protection Convention;

certain OECD Council recommendations concerning transboundary pollution, see:

   1974 OECD Council Recommendation C(74)224 on Transfrontier Pollution (Annex Title D);

   1976 OECD Council Recommendation C(76)55(Final) on Equal Right of Access in Relation to Transfrontier Pollution (Annex para. 2);

   1977 OECD Council Recommendation C(77)28(Final) on Implementation of a Regime of Equal Right of Access and Non-Discrimination in relation to Transfrontier Pollution (Annex Title B);

   1978 OECD Council Recommendation C(78)77(Final) on Strengthening International Co-operation on Environmental Protection in Frontier Regions (Annex Title II);

1971 Council of Europe Committee of Ministers Resolution (71)5 on Air Pollution in Frontier Areas, Conclusions 19(2), 34 et seq.;

42(2) of the 1981 UNEP Conclusions of the Study on the Legal Aspects concerning the Environment related to Offshore Mining and Drilling within the Limits of National jurisdiction; and

Principle 14 of the 1978 UNEP Draft Principles of Conduct concerning Shared Natural Resources

which provide for, recognize or recommend a right of access (equal or equivalent to the right possessed by nationals of the State of origin) to the administrative or judicial authorities of the State of origin without, however, affecting the possibility, where previously existing, to start proceedings before the administrative or judicial authorities of the (potentially) affected State.

In certain international agreements States, however, have decided to confer *exclusive* jurisdiction on the courts of one country. This has particularly been the case in certain conventions which impose strict liability on the operators of nuclear installations for nuclear damage caused by nuclear incidents. Thus, according to Article 13(a) and (b) of the 1960 Paris Convention on Third Party Liability in the Field of Nuclear Energy, as amended in 1964, jurisdiction will lie only with the courts of the Party in whose territory the nuclear incident occurred, or, when this incident occurred outside the territory of a Party or the place of the nuclear incident cannot be determined with certainty, with the courts of the Party in whose territory the nuclear installation of the operator liable is situated. Similar provisions are to be found in Article 11(1) and (2) of the 1963 Vienna Convention on Civil Liability for Nuclear Damage. Apart from the wish to maintain uniformity in case law, yet another reason has induced the Parties to confer jurisdiction on the courts of only one country, viz. the necessity to guarantee that the maximum amount for which the operator may be held liable will not be exceeded and that this amount will be equitably apportioned among the victims of the nuclear incident.

The problem of the applicable law in civil proceedings has also to some extent been dealt with in international agreements or resolutions. The 1974 Nordic Environmental Protection Convention provides in Article 2 that the *permissibility* of environmentally harmful activities shall be determined by the law of the State of origin. According to Article 3(2), however, the question of the *compensation* is to be judged by rules not less favourable to the injured party than the rules of compensation of the State of origin, thus leaving open the possibility of applying a more favourable law of the State where the harm has been caused.

It should be noted that according to the 1974 OECD Council Recommendation mentioned above States of origin should grant (potential) foreign victims "no less favourable" treatment than accorded to persons affected by similar pollution in the State of origin. "Equivalent treatment" and "the same remedies" have been recommended in Principle 14 of the 1978 UNEP Draft Principles of Conduct on Shared Natural Resources. It appears that the OECD recommendations and UNEP Draft Principle 14 do not prescribe the applicable law but rather purport to lay down a certain minimum standard for the treatment to be accorded to foreign victims.

Support for the principle formulated above is further to be found in the 1979 IIL Athens Resolution on Pollution of Rivers and Lakes and International Law (Article 7(i)) and in the 1982 ILA Montreal Rules on Water Pollution in an International Drainage Basin (Article 8).

Proceedings in the (potentially) affected State

The administrative law of a (potentially) affected State usually does not apply to environmentally harmful activities which take place outside its territory. Resort to the administrative authorities or courts of a State in which the harmful consequences of a certain transboundary environmental interference will be or are likely to be sustained will, therefore, usually be meaningless.

As we have seen, under the applicable national rules of private international law, civil proceedings can sometimes be brought only before the courts in the State of origin, sometimes only before the courts of the (potentially) affected State. We saw, moreover, that under the 1968 EC Jurisdiction and Enforcement of Judgments Convention, the courts of both the State of origin and the (potentially) affected State would be competent. In the discussion of the jurisdiction of the courts of the State of origin, reference was made to certain international agreements conferring *exclusive* jurisdiction on the courts of one State only. There are also certain international agreements imposing (strict) liability in which the courts of the State where the damage is sustained have been appointed as the—albeit not always exclusively—competent courts. For example, according to Article 11 of the 1969 Brussels International Convention on Civil Liability for Oil Pollution Damage, an action for compensation under the convention may be brought only before the courts of the State(s) in whose territory, including the territorial sea, the pollution damage has been caused. Another example is Article 11 of the 1976 London Convention on Civil Liability for Oil Pollution Damage Resulting from Exploration for and Exploitation of Seabed Mineral Resources, which provides that action for compensation under the convention may be brought only in the courts of a State where pollution damage was suffered as a result of an incident or in the courts of the so-called controlling State.

As we have seen, the law to be applied in civil proceedings—i.e. the law of the State of origin or the law of the (potentially) affected State—may vary depending on the rule of private international law of the forum State.

A considerable problem which may arise in cases before the courts of the (potentially) affected State is how a judgment rendered in favour of the plaintiff can be enforced. The plaintiff may have gained very little with the judgment in his favour, unless he succeeds in having the judgment enforced in the State where the polluting activities are undertaken and/or where the defendant possesses assets. The condition under which States are prepared to enforce judgments rendered by the courts of other States vary from one country to another. Obstacles for such an enforcement may be the lack of so-called "international" jurisdiction on the part of the court which rendered the judgment, i.e. that the court which rendered the judgment was, according to standards of the State considering enforcement, not competent to decide the case. Another obstacle to enforcement may be that the reciprocity requirement has not been satisfied or that the judgment will be regarded as incompatible with the "public policy" or "ordre public" of the State in which enforcement of the judgment is sought. Another factor to be kept in mind is, whether, and if so to what extent, the authorities of the

State considering enforcement of a foreign judgment will reconsider the merits of the case.

The above-mentioned difficulties may be considerably reduced when the States concerned have entered into a convention regulating the reciprocal recognition and enforcement of the judgments of their courts. Here again the 1968 EC Jurisdiction and Enforcement of Judgments Convention should be mentioned. According to that Convention, a contracting State may refuse the enforcement of a judgment rendered in another contracting State only on a limited number of grounds, the most important of these being that the decision shall not be contrary to the public policy of the State in which the enforcement is sought (see Articles 27, 28 and 34).

International non-intergovernmental proceedings

States may also create *international* non-intergovernmental proceedings to which persons who (may) create a transboundary interference or (potentially) affected persons may have (to take) resort. This approach has already been followed in the 1922 Agreement between Denmark and Germany relating to Watercourses and Dikes on the Danish—German Frontier. More recently, it was adopted in the 1971 Frontier Rivers Agreement concluded between Finland and Sweden. The agreement establishes the so-called Frontier Rivers Commission to which individuals may have resort to protect their interests against interferences originating in the territory of the other State. Activities which may result in transboundary pollution may only be conducted with a permit from the Commission. The law governing the activities covered by the agreement is, firstly, the provisions laid down in the agreement and secondly, the law prevailing in the two States. Except for certain questions as to which appeal is possible to a water rights court of appeal of either the State of origin or the (potentially) affected State, decisions of the Commission have immediate legal force. The agreement thus appears to take away many of the difficulties and disadvantages usually connected with the domestic approach.

The foregoing observations indicate that with regard to the *locus standi* of foreign victims, the competence of administrative or judicial authorities, the policy or law to be applied, and the enforceability of judgments rendered by foreign courts, many improvements are still to be made in many countries before foreign victims will possess adequate remedies against transboundary interferences. It is the clear objective of the principle in Article 20 to urge States to provide such remedies where these do not yet exist and to ensure that foreign victims will at least receive the same treatment as would be given to persons who would have been similarly affected within the State of origin.

STATE RESPONSIBILITY

Article 21

1. A State is responsible under international law for a breach of an international obligation relating to the use of a natural resource or the prevention or abatement of an environmental interference.

2. In particular, it shall:

(a) cease the internationally wrongful act;

(b) as far as possible, re-establish the situation which would have existed if the internationally wrongful act had not taken place;

(c) provide compensation for the harm which results from the internationally wrongful act;

(d) where appropriate, give satisfaction for the internationally wrongful act.

Comment

The principle formulated above is concerned with breaches of a State's obligations following from *binding* rules or principles of international law relating to the use of a natural resource (transboundary and/or otherwise) or the prevention or abatement of an environmental interference (transboundary and/or otherwise). It provides that in the event of a breach of such obligations, the State will incur so-called State responsibility, i.e. become answerable for the consequences which international law attaches to breaches of international law.

The notion of State responsibility must not be confused with the notion of strict liability under international law as used elsewhere in this report (see Article 11). While the rules and principles of international law regarding State responsibility (also called *secondary* rules and principles of international law) deal with the occurrence and the consequences of internationally *wrongful* acts, i.e. breaches of so-called *primary* rules or principles of international law, strict liability involves the financial accountability of States under international law for the harmful consequences of acts which are *not* unlawful under international law.

The principle of State responsibility for failure to comply with binding rules or principles of international law relating to the use of a (transboundary) natural resource or to a (transboundary) environmental interference has been explicitly recognized in:

(1) various international agreements (see the 1976 Barcelona Convention for the Mediterranean Sea (Article 12) and the 1982 UN Convention on the Law of the Sea (Articles 139(2) and 235(1));

(2) statements of intergovernmental bodies (see Principle 12 of the 1978 UNEP Draft Principles of Conduct on Shared National Resources); and

(3) non-intergovernmental international organizations (see the 1979 IIL Athens Resolution on Pollution of Rivers and Lakes and International Law (Article 5)).

Naturally one of the obligations arising from a continuing breach of a rule or principle of international law is the obligation to cease the unlawful conduct (see the 1966 ILA Helsinki Rules on the Uses of the Waters of International Rivers (Article 11(1)); 1972 ILA New York Rules on Marine Pollution of Continental Origin (Article 5); and 1982 ILA Montreal Rules on Water Pollution in an International Drainage Basin (Article 9)). It is, moreover, generally accepted that a State which has incurred State responsibility for a breach of an international obligation incumbent on it, is obliged "to make reparation". As stated by the Permanent Court of International Justice in the *Chorzów Factory case* this obligation results from "a principle of international law and even a general conception of law". In the same Judgment, the Court also indicated what this obligation actually amounted to. According to the Court:

> "That reparation must, in so far as possible, wipe out all the consequences of the illegal act and re-establish the situation which would, in all probability, have existed, if that act had not been committed. Restitution in kind, or, if that is not possible, payment of a sum corresponding to the value which a restitution in kind would bear, the award, if need be, of damages for loss sustained which would not be covered by restitution in kind or payment in place of it . . ."

In the passage just quoted the Court only mentioned *restitution* or *compensation* as modes of reparation, but it is generally accepted that reparation may also take the form of *satisfaction*.

Restitution in kind, specific restitution or *restitutio in integrum* purports to re-establish the situation which would have existed if the wrongful conduct had not taken place. It is this form of reparation to which the victim State appears to be primarily entitled, having regard to the statement quoted above of the Permanent Court of International Justice in the *Chorzów Factory case* "that reparation must, in so far as possible, wipe out all the consequences of the illegal act". Thus, restitution may, e.g. require measures to restore a depleted fish population or to clean the bed and banks of a watercourse. However, restitution is often not, or only partially, possible, or, when possible, is not requested by the injured State or is only capable of being effected by public authorities or persons in the injured State. In those cases compensation will be a proper remedy.

Compensation will usually be pecuniary compensation. However, nothing prohibits the States concerned from agreeing on compensation *in natura* and in practice this has been known to happen.

A duty of restitution and/or compensation exists only when there is a proper causal relationship between, on the one hand, the wrongful conduct and, on the other hand, the resultant damage. Stated more specifically, the wrongful conduct must not only have been the *conditio sine qua non* for the existence of the claimed item of damage, the damage must also have been the reasonably foreseeable and normal result of the wrongful conduct. This implies that damage which is "too remote" in the chain of causation or too speculative must be left out of consideration.

The duty to pay compensation has sometimes also been explicitly recognized in international agreements, viz. the 1948 Agreement concluded between Poland and the USSR concerning the Regime on the Soviet—Polish State Frontier (Article 14) or the 1960 Frontier Treaty concluded between the Federal Republic of Germany and the Netherlands (Article 63) or in resolutions of non-intergovernmental international organizations (see *supra* the 1966 ILA Helsinki Rules; 1972 ILA New York Rules and 1982 ILA Montreal Rules).

As was provided in Article 63(1) of the 1960 Frontier Treaty concluded between the Federal Republic of Germany and the Netherlands:

"If one of the Contracting Parties, notwithstanding the objections raised by the other Party, acts in violation of its obligations under this Chapter [on frontier waters] or arising under any of the special agreements to be concluded as provided in Article 59, thereby causing damage within the territory of the other Contracting Party, it shall be liable for damages."

Well known is the payment of compensation by Canada for the injury inflicted in the state of Washington in the United States by air pollution caused by a zinc and lead smelter in *Trail* (Canada). Under an agreement concluded in April 1935 Canada promised to pay $350,000 in payment of all damage which had occurred in the United States prior to 1 January 1932. The Arbitral Tribunal established by the two countries in 1935 found in its Interim Award of April 1938 that Canada had to pay another $78,000 for damage caused by the Trail Smelter in the United States in the period from 1 January 1932 up to 1 October 1937.

Another instance of a duty to pay compensation is to be found in the decision of the District Court of Rotterdam of December 1983 in the *Mines Domaniales de Potasse d'Alsace case*. Here the defendant was not State but state-owned potassium mines which were ordered to pay compensation for the transboundary harm caused to Dutch market gardeners as a result of the discharge by the defendant of waste salts into the Rhine in France. It is noteworthy that the court based its decision, inter alia, on an established breach of international law by the potassium mines.

A brief observation may finally be made on the third form of reparation besides *restitutio in integrum* and compensation, i.e. satisfaction. This constitutes a remedy for moral or political injury caused to another State. In contemporary international law and practice, satisfaction usually takes the form of a presentation of official regrets or apologies, of penal or disciplinary measures against guilty minor officials, or of a declaration by an international court or arbitral tribunal that an internationally wrongful act has been committed.

Satisfaction may also be called for in the case of a breach of a duty to prevent or abate environmental interferences of international importance, but it remains in such cases a remedy of minor importance.

PEACEFUL SETTLEMENT OF DISPUTES

Article 22

1. States, when they cannot avoid international disputes concerning the use of a natural resource or concerning an environmental interference in accordance with the preceding articles, shall settle such disputes by peaceful means in such a manner that international peace and security, and justice, are not endangered.

2. States shall accordingly seek a settlement of such disputes by negotiation, good offices, enquiry, mediation, conciliation, arbitration, judicial settlement, resort to appropriate bodies or arrangements, whether global or regional, or by any other peaceful means of their own choice.

3. In the event of a failure to reach a solution by another non-binding peaceful means within a period of 18 months after the dispute has arisen or within any other period of time agreed upon by the States

concerned, the dispute shall be submitted to conciliation at the request of any of the States concerned, unless it is agreed to proceed with an already agreed peaceful means or to submit the dispute to another binding or non-binding means of peaceful settlement.

4. In the event that the conciliation envisaged in Paragraph 3, or any other non-binding means of peaceful settlement resorted to in lieu thereof, does not lead to a solution of the dispute, the dispute shall be submitted to arbitration or judicial settlement at the request of any of the States concerned, unless it is agreed to submit the dispute to another means of peaceful settlement.

Comment

According to Article 2(3) of the Charter of the United Nations: "All Members shall settle their international disputes by peaceful means in such a manner that international peace and security, and justice, are not endangered." It is generally recognized that this principle embodies a well-established principle of international law, of which the application is not limited to Member States of the United Nations. The principle formulated in Paragraph 1 above merely restates this principle of international law, declaring it *expressis verbis* applicable to international disputes concerning the use of a natural resource or concerning an environmental interference when States have been unable to avoid such disputes by applying the preceding articles.

As indicated in Paragraph 2 there is a great variety of dispute settlement techniques available in international law and States are obliged to use one or more of these techniques with a view to settling their disputes. Having regard to the often highly technical nature of disputes concerning the use of a natural resource or the environment, fact-finding either in the form of enquiry or as an element of conciliation or arbitral or judicial settlement may be expected to play a dominant role.

As reaffirmed in UNGA Resolution No. 2625 (Annex) of 24 October 1970 on Principles of International Law concerning Friendly Relations and Co-operation among States in accordance with the Charter of the United Nations, the disputes must be settled on the basis of the sovereign equality of States and in accordance with the principle of free choice of means. Moreover, in case the parties to a dispute have not been able to arrive within a reasonable period of time at a solution by a certain dispute settlement procedure chosen by them, they shall continue to seek a settlement of the dispute by one of the other means of peaceful settlement of disputes available in international law.

However, in spite of the previously mentioned at present prevailing principle of free choice of means, it is believed that *de lege ferenda* there should exist a definite possibility for one or more of the States concerned to submit the dispute unilaterally to one or more specific means of settlement when it has not been possible to reach a settlement within a certain period of time by a commonly agreed means of settlement. Hence, it is proposed *de lege ferenda* in Paragraph 3 that, unless otherwise agreed, the dispute shall be submitted to conciliation at the request of any of the States concerned in the event of a failure to reach a solution by another non-binding means of settlement within a period of 18 months after the dispute has arisen or within any other period of time agreed upon by the States concerned. What has been said earlier (see the comment on Article 12) with regard to the time limit of 18 months is equally applicable here.

In the event that the conciliation envisaged in Paragraph 3 or any other non-binding means of peaceful settlement resorted to in lieu thereof, does not lead to a solution of the dispute, the dispute shall, unless otherwise agreed, in accordance with Paragraph 4, be submitted to arbitration or judicial settlement at the request of any of the States concerned.

Compulsory resort to conciliation involves an impartial investigation of the facts by the conciliation commission, followed by recommendations for a peaceful settlement of the dispute. In the present articles, conciliation serves as a final (if accepted by the parties to the dispute) or an intermediate (if not accepted by the parties) means of settlement, which differs from arbitration or judicial settlement in that the latter means lead to a third-party decision which is binding for the parties, while conciliation does not.

Conciliation as a means of peaceful settlement of disputes has been provided for in many international agreements, albeit not often in international agreements dealing specifically with the use of natural resources or the environment.

Examples of arrangements for arbitral and/or judicial settlement of disputes concerning the use of a natural resource or the environment are more frequently found, e.g. in:

1954 Convention concluded between Austria and Yugoslavia concerning Water Economy Questions relating to the Drava (Article 7);

1960 Frontier Treaty concluded between the Federal Republic of Germany and the Netherlands (Articles 67, 69 et seq.);

1960 Ems-Dollard Treaty concluded between the Federal Republic of Germany and the Netherlands (Article 50 et seq.);

1960 Paris Convention on Third Party Liability in the Field of Nuclear Energy (Article 17);

1965 Agreement between the Netherlands and the United Kingdom relating to the Exploitation of Single Geological Structures Extending across the Dividing Line on the Continental Shelf under the North Sea (Article 2);

1976 Bonn Convention on the Protection of the Rhine against Chemical Pollution (Article 15 and Annex B);

1976 Bonn Convention on the Protection of the Rhine against Pollution by Chlorides (Article 12 and Annex B); and, finally, the arbitral or judicial procedures provided for in the

1982 UN Convention on the Law of the Sea (Article 286 et seq.).

It may also be recalled that certain long-lasting disputes involving transboundary air pollution or diversion of the water of an international watercourse were finally settled by arbitration, viz. the *Trail Smelter Arbitration* (*United States* v. *Canada*) and the *Lake Lanoux Arbitration* (*Spain* v. *France*).

This proves that at least disputes relating to international or transboundary natural resources or environmental interferences may to some extent be submitted to binding peaceful settlement if the States concerned so agreed. In Paragraph 4 of the present article, such an agreement is not required and the provision in that paragraph must clearly be deemed to be *lex ferenda*. Still it is a provision worthwhile of being promoted. An alternative, less imaginative and attractive approach at least from the point of view of conserving natural resources and the environment, would be merely to oblige States to *seriously consider* the possibility of submitting the dispute to arbitration or judicial settlement in the event of a continued failure to reach a solution by any non-binding means within a reasonable time.

ANNEX

LIST OF INTERNATIONAL AGREEMENTS AND OTHER INSTRUMENTS

Most of the OECD Governments' Declarations or Council Recommendations referred to in this paper are to be found in *OECD and the Environment* (Paris, OECD, 1979).

The international agreements, resolutions, declarations or other instruments, etc., mentioned below have been listed in chronological order.

1906 Water Treaty concluded between Mexico and the United States (Convention concerning the Equitable Distribution of the Waters of the Rio Grande for

Irrigation), in: Martens NRGT 2nd Ser. Vol 35, p. 461, also in UN Doc. ST/LEG/SER.8/12 p. 232.

1909   Boundary Waters Treaty concluded between Great Britain (on behalf of Canada) and the United States, in: 4 AJIL 1910 Suppl. p. 239 or UN Doc. ST/LEG/SER.B/12 p. 260.

1911   Convention for the Preservation and Protection of Fur Seals, in: 104 BFSP p. 175.

1911   IIL Madrid Resolution on International Regulations regarding the Use of International Watercourses for Purposes other than Navigation, in: Annuaire Inst. Dr. Int. Vol 24 (1911) p. 365.

1922   Agreement relating to Watercourses and Dikes on the Danish–German Frontier concluded between Denmark and Germany, in: 10 LNTS p. 201.

1923   Convention for the Preservation of the Halibut Fishery of the Northern Pacific Ocean and the Bering Sea, in: 32 LNTS p. 94.

1929   Treaty of Peace, Friendship and Arbitration concluded between the Dominican Republic and Haiti, in: 105 LNTS p. 216.

1930   Convention for the Preservation of the Halibut Fishery of the Northern Pacific Ocean and the Bering Sea, in: 121 LNTS p. 46.

1931   Convention for the Regulation of Whaling, in: 155 LNTS p. 349.

1933   Montevideo Declaration concerning Industrial and Agricultural Use of International Rivers, in: UN Doc. A/5409 Vol III, Annex I pp. 2–4.

1937   (Revised) Convention for the Preservation of the Halibut Fishery of the Northern Pacific Ocean and the Bering Sea, in: 181 LNTS p. 209.

1940   Washington Convention on Nature Protection and Wild Life Preservation in the Western Hemisphere, in: 161 UNTS p. 193.

1944   Agreement relating to a Study to be Made by the International Joint Commission with respect to the Upper Columbia River Basin concluded between Canada and the United States, in: 109 UNTS p. 191.

1944   Water Treaty (Treaty relating to the Utilization of the Waters of the Colorado and Tijuana Rivers, and of the Rio Grande (Rio Bravo) from Fort Quitman (Texas), to the Gulf of Mexico), concluded between the United States and Mexico, in: 3 UNTS p. 314.

1946   International Convention for the Regulation of Whaling, in: 161 UNTS p. 72.

1946   London Convention for the Regulation of the Meshes of Fishing Nets and the Size Limits of Fish, in: 231 UNTS p. 200.

1948 Agreement concerning the Regime of the Soviet–Polish State Frontier concluded between Poland and the USSR, in 37 UNTS p. 66.

1949 Washington International Convention for the North-West Atlantic Fisheries, in: 157 UNTS p. 158.

1950 European Convention for the Protection of Human Rights and Fundamental Freedoms, in: 87 UNTS p. 103.

1950 Agreement regarding Co-operation in Meteorological and Hydrological Surveys in Certain Areas of the Nile Basin concluded between the United Kingdom (on behalf of Uganda) and Egypt, in: 226 UNTS p. 288.

1950 Paris International Convention for the Protection of Birds, in: 638 UNTS p. 185.

1952 Rome Convention on Damage Caused by Foreign Aircraft to Third Parties on the Surface, in: 310 UNTS p. 181.

1953 Convention for the Preservation of the Halibut Fishery of the Northern Pacific and the Bering Sea, in: 222 UNTS p. 77.

1954 Convention concerning Water Economy Questions relating to the Drava concluded between Austria and Yugoslavia, in: 227 UNTS p. 112.

1955 Agreement on Questions of Water Control, Water Control Systems and Frontier Waters concluded between Rumania and Yugoslavia, in: UN Doc. ST/LEG/SER.B/12 p. 928.

1957 Agreement on a Procedure and Plan for Co-operation in Making Hydro-economic Studies of the Drainage Area of Lake Dojran concluded between Greece and Yugoslavia, in: UN Doc. ST/LEG/SER.B/12 p. 813.

1957 Treaty Establishing the European Atomic Energy Community, in: 298 UNTS p. 167.

1957 Interim Convention on the Conservation of North Pacific Fur Seals, in: 314 UNTS p. 106.

1958 Agreement concerning a Study on the Utilization of the Water Power of the Apipe Falls concluded between Argentina and Paraguay, in: UN Doc. ST/LEG/SER.B/12 p. 156.

1958 UN Convention on Fishing and Conservation of the Living Resources of the High Seas, in: 559 UNTS p. 285.

1959 Nile Waters Agreement concluded between Egypt and the Sudan, in: 453 UNTS p. 51.

1959 Varna Convention concerning Fishing in the Black Sea, in: 377 UNTS p. 203.

1959   London North-East Atlantic Fisheries Convention, in: 486 UNTS p. 157.

1960   Ems-Dollard Treaty concluded between the Federal Republic of Germany and the Netherlands, in: Tractatenblad van het Koninkrijk der Nederlanden 1960 No. 69.

1960   Frontier Treaty concluded between the Federal Republic of Germany and the Netherlands, in: 508 UNTS p. 26.

1960   Paris Convention on Third Party Liability in the Field of Nuclear Energy, in: 55 AJIL 1961 p. 1083, amended by the 1964 Additional Protocol, in: Tractatenblad van het Koninkrijk der Nederlanden 1964 No. 178.

1960   Indus Waters Treaty concluded between India and Pakistan, in: 419 UNTS p. 125.

1960   Steckborn Convention on the Protection of Lake Constance against Pollution, in: UN Doc. ST/LEG/SER.B/12 p. 438.

1960   Treaty concerning the Improvement of the Terneuzen and Ghent Canal concluded between Belgium and the Netherlands, in: 432 UNTS p. 19.

1961   European Social Charter, in: Eur. Treaty Series No. 35.

1961   Treaty relating to Co-operative Development of the Water Resources of the Columbia River concluded between Canada and the United States, in: TIAS No. 5638.

1961   IIL Salzburg Resolution on the Use of International Non-Maritime Waters, in: Annuaire Inst. Dr. Int. Vol. 49 II (1961) pp. 381–384.

1962   Treaty of Co-operation between Denmark, Finland, Iceland, Norway and Sweden, in: 10 Eur. Yearbook p. 941.

1962   Brussels Convention on the Liability of Operators of Nuclear Ships, in: 57 AJIL 1963 p. 268.

1963   Berne Convention on the International Commission for the Protection of the Rhine against Pollution, in: Tractatenblad van het Koninkrijk der Nederlanden 1963 No. 104, amended: idem 1977 no. 31.

1963   Niamey Act regarding Navigation and Economic Co-operation between the States of the Niger Basin, in: 587 UNTS p. 9.

1963   Brussels Convention Supplementary to the 1960 Paris Convention on Third Party Liability in the Field of Nuclear Energy, in: 2 ILM 1963, p. 685.

1963   Vienna Convention on Civil Liability for Nuclear Damage, in: 2 ILM 1962, p. 727.

1963   Washington Protocol to the 1949 Washington International Convention for the North-West Atlantic Fisheries, in: 590 UNTS p. 292.

1964 Agreement concerning Frontier Watercourses concluded between Finland and the USSR, in: 537 UNTS p. 231.

1964 Agreement concerning the Use of Water Resources in Frontier Waters concluded between Poland and the USSR, in: 552 UNTS p. 175.

1964 Niamey Agreement concerning the River Niger Commission and the Navigation and Transport on the River Niger, in: 587 UNTS p. 19.

1964 Agreement concerning the Use of Water Resources in Frontier Waters concluded between Poland and the USSR, in: 552 UNTS p. 175.

1965 Agreement on Co-operation in Water Economy Questions in Frontier Waters concluded between the German Democratic Republic and Poland, in: German Dem. Rep. Gesetzblatt 1967 I p. 94.

1965 Agreement relating to the Exploitation of Single Geological Structures Extending Across the Dividing Line on the Continental Shelf under the North Sea concluded between the Netherlands and the United Kingdom, in: Tractatenblad van het Koninkrijk der Nederlanden 1965 No. 192.

1965 Draft Convention on the Industrial and Agricultural Use of International Rivers and Lakes prepared by the Inter-American Judicial Committee of the Organization of American States, in: OAS Doc. OEA/Ser. 1/VI.1, CIJ-83.

1966 Agreement on Radiologic Protection concerning the Installations of the Nuclear Power Station of the Ardennes concluded between France and Belgium, in: Moniteur belge of 7 March 1967 p. 2276.

1966 Agreement Regulating the Withdrawal of Water from Lake Constance concluded between Austria, the Federal Republic of Germany and Switzerland, in: 620 UNTS p. 191.

1966 UN Covenant on Civil and Political Rights, in: Annex to UNGA Resolution 2200 (XXI) of 16 December 1966, also in: 6 ILM 1967 p. 368.

1966 UN Covenant on Economic, Social and Cultural Rights, in: Annex to UNGA Resolution 2200 (XXI) of 16 December 1966, also in: 6 ILM 1967 p. 360.

1966 Rio de Janeiro International Convention for the Conservation of Atlantic Tunas, in: 673 UNTS p. 63.

1966 ILA Helsinki Rules on the Uses of the Waters of International Rivers, in: International Law Association, 52nd Conf. Rep. (1967) p. 484.

1968 European Agreement on the Restriction of the Use of Certain Detergents in Washing and Cleaning Products, in: Eur. Treaty Ser. No. 64.

1968 Agreement concerning Co-operation in the Use of the Waters of Rivers

Flowing through the Territory of Both Countries concluded between Bulgaria and Turkey, in: 807 UNTS p. 117.

1968   EC Convention on Jurisdiction and Enforcement of Judgments in Civil and Commercial Matters, in: Off. Jl. Eur. Com. 1978 L 304.

1968   African Convention on the Conservation of Nature and Natural Resources, in: Int. Env. Law 968: 68/2.

1969   Rome Convention on the Conservation of the Living Resources of the South-East Atlantic, in: 801 UNTS p. 10.

1969   Bonn Agreement for Co-operation in Dealing with Water Pollution of the North Sea by Oil. in: 9 ILM 1970 p. 359.

1969   Brussels International Convention on Civil Liability for Oil Pollution Damage, in: 9 ILM 1969, p. 45.

1970   EEC Directive on the Approximation of the Laws of the Member States relating to Measures to be Taken against Air Pollution by Gases from Positive-Ignition Engines of Motor Vehicles, in: Off. Jl. Eur. Com. 1970 L. 76.

1971   Ramsar Convention on Wetlands of International Importance, Especially as Water Fowl Habitat, in: 11 ILM 1972 p. 969.

1971   Frontier Rivers Agreement concluded between Finland and Sweden, in: 825 UNTS p. 191.

1971   Act of Santiago concerning Hydrologic Basins adopted between Argentina and Chile, in: UN Doc. A/CN.4/274 Vol I p. 180.

1971   Buenos Aires Declaration on Water Resources adopted by Argentina and Uruguay, in: UN Doc. A/CN.4/274 Vol I p. 181.

1971   Council of Europe Committee of Ministers Resolution (71) 5 on Air Pollution in Frontier Areas, in: 19 Eur. Yb. 1971 p. 263.

1971   Declaration of Asunción on the Use of International Rivers adopted by the Ministers for Foreign Affairs of the countries of the La Plata River Basin (Argentina, Bolivia, Brazil, Paraguay and Uruguay), in: UN Doc. A/CN.4/274 Vol I p. 178.

1972   Convention on Liability for Damage Caused by Objects Launched into Outer Space, in: 10 ILM 1971, p. 965 and 11 ILM 1972 p. 250.

1972   London Convention for the Conservation of Antarctic Seals, in: 11 ILM 1972 p. 251.

1972   Oslo Convention for the Prevention of Marine Pollution by Dumping from Ships and Aircraft, in: 11 ILM 1972 p. 262.

1972 Agreement on Co-operation in the Field of Environmental Protection concluded between the United States and the USSR, in: 11 ILM 1972 p. 761.

1972 Convention on the Prevention of Marine Pollution by Dumping of Wastes and Other Matter, in: 11 ILM 1972 p. 1294.

1972 Paris Convention concerning the Protection of World Cultural and Natural Heritage, in: 11 ILM 1972 p. 1358.

1972 UN Declaration on the Human Environment, in: UN Doc. A/CONF.48/14.

1972 ILA New York Rules on Marine Pollution of Continental Origin, in: International Law Association, 55th Conf. Rep. pp. xvii–xviii, see also pp. 98–105.

1973 Washington Convention on International Trade in Endangered Species of Wild Fauna and Flora, in: 12 ILM 1973 p. 1088.

1973 Agreement concerning the Permanent and Definitive Solution to the International Problem of the Salinity of the Colorado River concluded between Mexico and the United States, in: 12 ILM 1973 p. 1105.

1973 Agreement concerning the Prevention and Abatement of Injurious Incidences in the Frontier Area concluded between the Federal Republic of Germany and the German Democratic Republic, in: Bundesgesetzblatt 1974 II p. 1238 (Federal Republic of Germany).

1973 Gdansk Convention on Fishing and Conservation of the Living Resources in the Baltic Sea and the Belts, in: 12 ILM 1973 p. 1292.

1973 London International Convention for the Prevention of Pollution from Ships, in: 12 ILM 1973 p. 1319.

1973 Oslo Agreement on the Conservation of Polar Bears, in: 13 ILM 1974 p. 13.

1973 Treaty concerning the La Plata River and its Maritime Limits concluded between Argentina and Uruguay, in: 13 ILM 1974 p. 251.

1973 EC Programme of Action on the Environment, in: Off. Jl. Eur. Com. 1973 C 112.

1973 EEC Council Directive on the Approximation of the Laws of the Member States relating to Detergents, in: Off. Jl. Eur. Com. 1973 L. 347.

1973 Draft Propositions on the Law of International Rivers proposed by a subcommittee of the Asian-African Legal Consultative Committee, in: UN Doc A/CN.4/274 Vol II p. 226.

1974 Agreement concerning Water Economy Questions in Frontier Waters concluded between the German Democratic Republic and Czechoslovakia, in:

Sozialistische Landeskultur Umweltschutz, Textausgabe ausgewählter Rechtsvorschriften, Staatsverslag der Deutsch. Dem. Rep., Berlin 1978, p. 375.

1974   Helsinki Convention for the Protection of the Marine Environment of the Baltic Sea Area, in: 13 ILM 1974 p. 546.

1974   Nordic Environmental Protection Convention, in: 13 ILM 1974 p. 591.

1974   Paris Convention for the Prevention of Marine Pollution from Land-Based Sources, in: 13 ILM 1974 p. 352.

1974   Agreement on Co-operation in Environmental Affairs concluded between the United States and the Federal Republic of Germany, in: 13 ILM 1974 p. 598.

1975   Agreement on the Exchange of Information on Weather Modification Activities concluded between Canada and the United States, in: 14 ILM 1975 p. 589.

1975   EEC Council Directive relating to the Sulphur Content of Gas Oils, in: Off. Jl. Eur. Com. 1975 L. 307.

1975   Final Act of the Conference on Security and Co-operation in Europe, in: 14 ILM 1975 p. 1292.

1976   Barcelona Convention for the Protection of the Mediterranean Sea against Pollution, in: 15 ILM 1976, p. 290.

1976   Bonn Convention on the Protection of the Rhine against Chemical Pollution, in: 16 ILM 1977 p. 242.

1976   Bonn Convention on the Protection of the Rhine against Pollution by Chlorides, in: 16 ILM 1977 p. 265.

1976   London Convention on Civil Liability for Oil Pollution Damage Resulting from Exploration for and Exploitation of Seabed Mineral Resources, in: 16 ILM 1977, p. 1450.

1976   Apia Convention on the Conservation of Nature in the South Pacifiic, in: UNEP Reference Series 3, Selected Multilateral Treaties in the Field of the Environment, ed. A. Ch. Kiss, UNEP Nairobi 1983 pp. 47, 463.

1976   Washington Convention on the Conservation of North Pacific Fur Seals, in: UNEP References series 3, selected Multilateral Treaties in the Field of the Environment, ed. A. Ch. Kiss, UNEP Nairobi 1983 pp. 47, 460.

1976   EEC Council Directive on Pollution Caused by Certain Dangerous Substances Discharged into the Aquatic Environment of the Community, in: Off. Jl. Eur. Com. 1976 L. 129.

1976 ILA Madrid Resolution on the Protection of Water Resources and Water Installations in Times of Armed Conflict, in: International Law Association, 57th Conf. Rep. (1978) p. xxxv.

1976 ILA Madrid Resolution on International Water Resources Administration, in: International Law Association, 57th Conf. Rep. (1978) p. 37.

1977 Geneva Convention on the Prohibition of Military or Any Other Hostile Use of Environmental Modification Techniques, in: 16 ILM 1977 p. 88.

1977 Agreement relating to Exchange of Information on Construction of Nuclear Installations along the Border concluded between Denmark and the Federal Republic of Germany, in: 17 ILM 1978 p. 274.

1978 Brasilia Treaty for Amazonian Co-operation, in: 17 ILM 1978 p. 1045.

1978 Great Lakes Water Quality Agreement concluded between Canada and the United States, in: TIAS No. 9257.

1978 Kuwait Regional Convention for Co-operation on the Protection of the Marine Environment from Pollution, in: 17 ILM 1978 p. 511.

1978 UNEP Draft Principles of Conduct in the Field of the Environment for the Guidance of States in the Conservation and Harmonious Utilization of Natural Resources Shared by Two or More States, in: 17 ILM 1978 p. 1097.

1979 Berne Convention on the Conservation of European Wildlife and Natural Habitats, in: Eur. Treaty Series No. 104.

1979 Bonn Convention on the Conservation of Migratory Species of Wild Animals, in: 19 ILM 1980 p. 15.

1979 ECE Convention on Long-Range Transboundary Air Pollution, in: 18 ILM 1979 p. 1442.

1979 IIL Athens Resolution on Pollution of Rivers and Lakes and International Law, in: Annuaire Inst. Dr. Int. Vol 58 I (1980) p. 197.

1980 Athens Protocol (for the Protection of the Mediterranean Sea against Pollution from Land-Based Sources) to the 1976 Barcelona Convention for the Protection of the Mediterranean Sea, in: 19 ILM 1980 p. 869.

1980 Agreement concerning a Norwegian-Finnish Commission for Frontier Watercourses, in: Overenskomster med fremede stater 1981 p. 236 (Norway).

1980 Memorandum of Intent on Transboundary Air Pollution concluded between Canada and the United States, in: 20 ILM 1981 p. 690.

1980   EEC Council Directive on Air Quality Limit Values and Guide Values for Sulphur Dioxide and Suspended Particulates, in: Off. Jl. Eur. Com. 1980 L 229.

1980   ECE Declaration of Policy on Prevention and Control of Water Pollution, Including Transboundary Pollution, in: 6 Env. Pol. and Law 1980 pp. 148–150.

1980   Declaration of Environmental Policies and Procedures relating to Economic Development adopted by the African Development Bank, the Arab Bank for Economic Development in Africa, the Asian Development Bank, the World Bank, the Commission of the European Community, the OAS, UNDP and UNEP, in: 19 ILM 1980 p. 524.

1980   World Conservation Strategy, Living Resources Conservation for Sustainable Development, prepared by IUCN in co-operation with UNEP, WWF, FAO and UNESCO, 1980.

1980   ILA Belgrade Articles on the Regulation of the Flow of Water of International Watercourses, in: International Law Association, 59th Conf. Rep. p. 362.

1981   Abidjan Convention for Co-operation in the Protection and Development of the Marine Environment of the West and Central African Region, in: 20 ILM 1981 p. 746.

1981   Lima Convention for the Protection of the Marine Environment and Coastal Areas of the South-East Pacific, in: UNEP, Convention for the Protection of the Marine Environment and Coastal Areas of the South-East Pacific and its Supplementary Agreements (New York 1984).

1981   Convention concerning Water Economy Questions in Frontier Waters concluded between Hungary and the USSR, in: Törvények és rendeletek hivalatos gyüjteménye (Hungary).

1981   Atlantic Treaty Consultative Meeting Recommendation XI-I on Antarctic Mineral Resources, in: 20 ILM 1981 p. 1265.

1981   UNEP Conclusions of the Study on the Legal Aspects concerning the Environment related to Offshore Mining and Drilling within the Limits of National Jurisdiction, in: UN Doc. UNEP/GC.9/5/Add. 5 Annex III (1981), also in: 7 Env. Pol. and Law 1981 p. 50.

1982   Jeddah Regional Convention for the Conservation of the Regional Environment of the Red Sea and Gulf of Aden, in: 9 Env. Pol. and Law 1982 p. 56.

1982   UN Law of the Sea Convention, in: 21 ILM 1982 p. 1261.

1982   EEC Council Directive on Major Accident Hazards of Certain Industrial Activities, in: Off. Jl. Eur. Com. 1982 L. 230.

1982   EEC Council Directive on Air Quality Limit Value for Lead, in: Off. Jl. Eur. Com. 1982 L. 378.

1982   UNEP Gov. Council Nairobi Declaration, in: 21 ILM 1982 p. 676.

1982   New York–Quebec Agreement on Acid Precipitation, in: 21 ILM 1982 p. 721.

1982   ILA Montreal Rules of International Law Applicable to Transfrontier Pollution, in: International Law Association, 60th Conf. Rep. p. 1.

1982   ILA Montreal Rules on Water Pollution in an International Drainage Basin, in: International Law Association, 60th Conf. Rep. p. 535.

1983   Agreement on Co-operation for the Protection and Improvement of the Environment in the Border Area concluded between Mexico and the United States, in: 22 ILM 1983 p. 1025.

1983   Agreement to Track Air Pollution across Eastern North America concluded between Canada and the United States, in: 22 ILM 1983 p. 1017.

1983   Cartagena de Indias Convention for the Protection and Development of the Marine Environment of the Wider Caribbean Region, in: 22 ILM 1983 p. 227.

1984   ECA Council of Ministers Resolution on Environment and Development in Africa, in: UN Doc. E/ECAA/CM. 10/38.

1985   ASEAN Agreement on the Conservation of Nature and Natural Resources, in: 15 Env. Pol and Law 1985.

1985   EEC Council Directive on the Assessment of the Effects of Certain Public and Private Projects on the Environment, in: Off. Jl. Eur. Com. 1985 L 175.

ANNEX I

SELECTED REFERENCE DOCUMENTS

CONTENTS

DECLARATION OF THE UNITED NATIONS CONFERENCE ON THE HUMAN ENVIRONMENT*

Stockholm, 16 June 1972

The United Nations Conference on the Human Environment

Having met at Stockholm from 5 to 16 June 1972,
Having considered the need for a common outlook and for common principles to inspire and guide the peoples of the world in the preservation and enhancement of the human environment,

I

Proclaims that:

1. Man is both creature and moulder of his environment, which gives him physical sustenance and affords him the opportunity for intellectual, moral, social and spiritual growth. In the long and tortuous evolution of the human race on this planet a stage has been reached when, through the rapid acceleration of science and technology, man has acquired the power to transform his environment in countless ways and on an unprecedented scale. Both aspects of man's environment, the natural and the man-made, are essential to his well-being and to the enjoyment of basic human rights—even the right to life itself.

2. The protection and improvement of the human environment is a major issue which affects the well-being of peoples and economic development

*In: UN DOC A/CONF. 48/14 p. 2 et seq.

throughout the world; it is the urgent desire of the peoples of the whole world and the duty of all Governments.

3. Man has constantly to sum up experience and go on discovering, inventing, creating and advancing. In our time, man's capability to transform his surroundings, if used wisely, can bring to all peoples the benefits of development and the opportunity to enhance the quality of life. Wrongly or heedlessly applied, the same power can do incalculable harm to human beings and the human environment. We see around us growing evidence of man-made harm in many regions of the earth: dangerous levels of pollution in water, air, earth and living beings; major and undesirable disturbances to the ecological balance of the biosphere; destruction and depletion of irreplaceable resources; and gross deficiencies harmful to the physical, mental and social health of man, in the man-made environment, particularly in the living and working environment.

4. In the developing countries most of the environmental problems are caused by under-development. Millions continue to live far below the minimum levels required for a decent human existence, deprived of adequate food and clothing, shelter and education, health and sanitation. Therefore, the developing countries must direct their efforts to development, bearing in mind their priorities and the need to safeguard and improve the environment. For the same purpose, the industrialized countries should make efforts to reduce the gap between themselves and the developing countries. In the industrialized countries, environmental problems are generally related to industrialization and technological development.

5. The natural growth of population continuously presents problems on the preservation of the environment, and adequate policies and measures should be adopted, as appropriate, to face these problems. Of all things in the world, people are the most precious. It is the people that propel social progress, create social wealth, develop science and technology and, through their hard work, continuously transform the human environment. Along with social progress and the advance of production, science and technology, the capability of man to improve the environment increases with each passing day.

6. A point has been reached in history when we must shape our actions throughout the world with a more prudent care for their environmental consequences. Through ignorance or indifference we can do massive and irreversible harm to the earthly environment on which our life and well-being depend. Conversely, through fuller knowledge and wiser action, we can achieve for ourselves and our posterity a better life in an environment more in keeping with human needs and hopes. There are broad vistas for the

enhancement of environmental quality and the creation of a good life. What is needed is an enthusiastic but calm state of mind and intense but orderly work. For the purpose of attaining freedom in the world of nature, man must use knowledge to build, in collaboration with nature, a better environment. To defend and improve the human environment for present and future generations has become an imperative goal for mankind—a goal to be pursued together with, and in harmony with, the established and fundamental goals of peace and of world-wide economic and social development.

7. To achieve this environmental goal will demand the acceptance of responsibility by citizens and communities and by enterprises and institutions at every level, all sharing equitably in common efforts. Individuals in all walks of life as well as organizations in many fields, by their values and the sum of their actions, will shape the world environment of the future. Local and national governments will bear the greatest burden for large-scale environmental policy and action within their jurisdictions. International co-operation is also needed in order to raise resources to support the developing countries in carrying out their responsibilities in this field. A growing class of environmental problems, because they are regional or global in extent or because they affect the common international realm, will require extensive co-operation among nations and action by international organizations in the common interest. The Conference calls upon Governments and peoples to exert common efforts for the preservation and improvement of the human environment, for the benefit of all the people and for their posterity.

II

Principles

States the common conviction that:

Principle 1

Man has the fundamental right to freedom, equality and adequate conditions of life, in an environment of a quality that permits a life of dignity and well-being, and he bears a solemn responsibility to protect and improve the environment for present and future generations. In this respect, policies promoting or perpetuating *apartheid*, racial segregation, discrimination, colonial and other forms of oppression and foreign domination stand condemned and must be eliminated.

Principle 2

The natural resources of the earth including the air, water, land, flora and fauna and especially representative samples of natural ecosystems must be safeguarded for the benefit of present and future generations through careful planning or management, as appropriate.

Principle 3

The capacity of the earth to produce vital renewable resources must be maintained and, wherever practicable, restored or improved.

Principle 4

Man has a special responsibility to safeguard and wisely manage the heritage of wildlife and its habitat which are now gravely imperilled by a combination of adverse factors. Nature conservation including wildlife must therefore receive importance in planning for economic development.

Principle 5

The non-renewable resources of the earth must be employed in such a way as to guard against the danger of their future exhaustion and to ensure that benefits from such employment are shared by all mankind.

Principle 6

The discharge of toxic substances or of other substances and the release of heat, in such quantities or concentrations as to exceed the capacity of the environment to render them harmless, must be halted in order to ensure that serious or irreversible damage is not inflicted upon ecosystems. The just struggle of the peoples of all countries against pollution should be supported.

Principle 7

States shall take all possible steps to prevent pollution of the seas by substances that are liable to create hazards to human health, to harm living resources and marine life, to damage amenities or to interfere with other legitimate uses of the sea.

Principle 8

Economic and social development is essential for ensuring a favourable living and working environment for man and for creating conditions on earth that are necessary for the improvement of the quality of life.

Principle 9

Environmental deficiencies generated by the conditions of underdevelopment and natural disasters pose grave problems and can best be remedied by accelerated development through the transfer of substantial quantities of financial and technological assistance as a supplement to the domestic effort of the developing countries and such timely assistance as may be required.

Principle 10

For the developing countries, stability of prices and adequate earnings for primary commodities and raw material are essential to environmental management since economic factors as well as ecological processes must be taken into account.

Principle 11

The environmental policies of all States should enhance and not adversely affect the present or future development potential of developing countries, nor should they hamper the attainment of better living conditions for all, and appropriate steps should be taken by States and international organizations with a view to reaching agreement on meeting the possible national and international economic consequences resulting from the application of environmental measures.

Principle 12

Resources should be made available to preserve and improve the environment, taking into account the circumstances and particular requirements of developing countries and any costs which may emanate from their incorporating environmental safeguards into their development planning and the need for making available to them, upon their request, additional international technical and financial assistance for this purpose.

Principle 13

In order to achieve a more rational management of resources and thus to improve the environment, States should adopt an integrated and co-ordinated approach to their development planning so as to ensure that development is compatible with the need to protect and improve the human environment for the benefit of their population.

Principle 14

Rational planning constitutes an essential tool for reconciling any conflict between the needs of development and the need to protect and improve the environment.

Principle 15

Planning must be applied to human settlements and urbanization with a view to avoiding adverse effects on the environment and obtaining maximum social, economic and environmental benefits for all. In this respect projects which are designed for colonialist and racist domination must be abandoned.

Principle 16

Demographic policies, which are without prejudice to basic human rights and which are deemed appropriate by Governments concerned, should be applied in those regions where the rate of population growth or excessive population concentrations are likely to have adverse effects on the environment or development, or where low population density may prevent improvement of the human environment and impede development.

Principle 17

Appropriate national institutions must be entrusted with the task of planning, managing or controlling the environmental resources of States with the view to enhancing environmental quality.

Principle 18

Science and technology, as part of their contribution to economic and social development, must be applied to the identification, avoidance and control of environmental risks and the solution of environmental problems and for the common good of mankind.

Principle 19

Education in environmental matters, for the younger generation as well as adults, giving due consideration to the underprivileged, is essential in order to broaden the basis for an enlightened opinion and responsible conduct by individuals, enterprises and communities in protecting and improving the environment in its full human dimension. It is also essential that mass media of communications avoid contributing to the deterioration of the environment, but, on the contrary, disseminate information of an educational nature, on the need to protect and improve the environment in order to enable man to develop in every respect.

Principle 20

Scientific research and development in the context of environmental problems, both national and multinational, must be promoted in all countries, especially the developing countries. In this connexion, the free flow of up-to-date scientific information and transfer of experience must be supported and assisted, to facilitate the solution of environmental problems; environmental technologies should be made available to developing countries on terms which would encourage their wide dissemination without constituting an economic burden on the developing countries.

Principle 21

States have, in accordance with the Charter of the United Nations and the principles of international law, the sovereign right to exploit their own resources pursuant to their own environmental policies, and the responsibility to ensure that activities within their jurisdiction or control do not cause damage to the environment of other States or of areas beyond the limits of national jurisdiction.

Principle 22

States shall co-operate to develop further the international law regarding liability and compensation for the victims of pollution and other environmental damage caused by activities within the jurisdiction or control of such States to areas beyond their jurisdiction.

Principle 23

Without prejudice to such criteria as may be agreed upon by the international community, or to standards which will have to be determined nationally, it will be essential in all cases to consider the systems of values prevailing in each country, and the extent of the applicability of standards which are valid for the most advanced countries but which may be inappropriate and of unwarranted social cost for the developing countries.

Principle 24

International matters concerning the protection and improvement of the environment should be handled in a co-operative spirit by all countries, big or small, on an equal footing. Co-operation through multilateral or bilateral arrangements or other appropriate means is essential to effectively control, prevent, reduce and eliminate adverse environmental effects resulting from activities conducted in all spheres, in such a way that due account is taken of the sovereignty and interests of all States.

Principle 25

States shall ensure that international organizations play a co-ordinated, efficient and dynamic role for the protection and improvement of the environment.

Principle 26

Man and his environment must be spared the effects of nuclear weapons and all other means of mass destruction. States must strive to reach prompt agreement, in the relevant international organs, on the elimination and complete destruction of such weapons.

UN GENERAL ASSEMBLY RESOLUTION ON THE WORLD CHARTER FOR NATURE*

New York, 28 October 1982

The General Assembly,

Reaffirming the fundamental purposes of the United Nations, in particular the maintenance of international peace and security, the development of friendly relations among nations and the achievement of international co-operation in solving international problems of an economic, social, cultural, technical, intellectual or humanitarian character,

Aware that:

(a) Mankind is a part of nature and life depends on the uninterrupted functioning of natural systems which ensure the supply of energy and nutrients,

(b) Civilization is rooted in nature, which has shaped human culture and influenced all artistic and scientific achievement, and living in harmony with nature gives man the best opportunities for the development of his creativity, and for rest and recreation,

Convinced that:

(a) Every form of life is unique, warranting respect regardless of its worth to man, and, to accord other organisms such recognition, man must be guided by a moral code of action,

(b) Man can alter nature and exhaust natural resources by his action or its consequences and, therefore, must fully recognize the urgency of maintaining the stability and quality of nature and of conserving natural resources,

Persuaded that:

(a) Lasting benefits from nature depend upon the maintenance of essential ecological processes and life support systems, and upon the diversity of life

---

*UN General Assembly Res. No. 37/7 adopted on 28 October 1982.

forms, which are jeopardized through excessive exploitation and habitat destruction by man,

(b) The degradation of natural systems owing to excessive consumption and misuse of natural resources, as well as to failure to establish an appropriate economic order among peoples and among States, leads to the breakdown of the economic, social and political framework of civilization,

(c) Competition for scarce resources creates conflicts, whereas the conservation of nature and natural resources contributes to justice and the maintenance of peace and cannot be achieved until mankind learns to live in peace and to forsake war and armaments,

Reaffirming that man must acquire the knowledge to maintain and enhance his ability to use natural resources in a manner which ensures the preservation of the species and ecosystems for the benefit of present and future generations,

Firmly convinced of the need for appropriate measures, at the national and international, individual and collective, and private and public levels, to protect nature and promote international co-operation in this field,

Adopts, to these ends, the present World Charter for Nature, which proclaims the following principles of conservation by which all human conduct affecting nature is to be guided and judged.

I. General Principles

1. Nature shall be respected and its essential processes shall not be impaired.

2. The genetic viability on the earth shall not be compromised; the population levels of all life forms, wild and domesticated, must be at least sufficient for their survival, and to this end necessary habitats shall be safeguarded.

3. All areas of the earth, both land and sea, shall be subject to these principles of conservation; special protection shall be given to unique areas, to representative samples of all different types of ecosystems and to the habitats of rare or endangered species.

4. Ecosystems and organisms, as well as the land, marine and atmospheric resources that are utilized by man, shall be managed to achieve and maintain

optimum sustainable productivity, but not in such a way as to endanger the integrity of those other ecosystems or species with which they coexist.

5. Nature shall be secured against degradation caused by warfare or other hostile activities.

II. Functions

6. In the decisionmaking process it shall be recognized that man's needs can be met only by ensuring the proper functioning of natural systems and by respecting the principles set forth in the present Charter.

7. In the planning and implementation of social and economic development activities, due account shall be taken of the fact that the conservation of nature is an integral part of those activities.

8. In formulating long-term plans for economic development, population growth and the improvement of standards of living, due account shall be taken of the long-term capacity of natural systems to ensure the subsistence and settlement of the populations concerned, recognizing that this capacity may be enhanced through science and technology.

9. The allocation of areas of the earth to various uses shall be planned, and due account shall be taken of the physical constraints, the biological productivity and diversity and the natural beauty of the areas concerned.

10. Natural resources shall not be wasted, but used with a restraint appropriate to the principles set forth in the present Charter, in accordance with the following rules:

(a) Living resources shall not be utilized in excess of their natural capacity for regeneration;

(b) The productivity of soils shall be maintained or enhanced through measures which safeguard their long-term fertility and the process of organic decomposition, and prevent erosion and all other forms of degradation;

(c) Resources, including water, which are not consumed as they are used shall be reused or recycled;

(d) Non-renewable resources which are consumed as they are used shall be exploited with restraint, taking into account their abundance, the rational possibilities of converting them for consumption, and the compatibility of their exploitation with the functioning of natural systems.

11. Activities which might have an impact on nature shall be controlled,

and the best available technologies that minimize significant risks to nature or other adverse effects shall be used; in particular:

(a) Activities which are likely to cause irreversible damage to nature shall be avoided;

(b) Activities which are likely to pose a significant risk to nature shall be preceded by an exhaustive examination; their proponents shall demonstrate that expected benefits outweigh potential damage to nature, and where potential adverse effects are not fully understood, the activities should not proceed;

(c) Activities which may disturb nature shall be preceded by assessment of their consequences, and environmental impact studies of development projects shall be conducted sufficiently in advance, and if they are to be undertaken, such activities shall be planned and carried out so as to minimize potential adverse effects;

(d) Agriculture, grazing, forestry and fisheries practices shall be adapted to the natural characteristics and constraints of given areas;

(e) Areas degraded by human activities shall be rehabilitated for purposes in accord with their natural potential and compatible with the well-being of affected populations.

12. Discharge of pollutants into natural systems shall be avoided and:

(a) Where this is not feasible, such pollutants shall be treated at the source, using the best practicable means available;

(b) special precautions shall be taken to prevent discharge of radioactive or toxic wastes.

13. Measures intended to prevent, control or limit natural disasters, infestations and diseases shall be specifically directed to the causes of these scourges and shall avoid adverse side-effects on nature.

III. Implementation

14. The principles set forth in the present Charter shall be reflected in the law and practice of each State, as well as at the international level.

15. Knowledge of nature shall be broadly disseminated by all possible means, particularly by ecological education as an integral part of general education.

16. All planning shall include, among its essential elements, the formulation of strategies for the conservation of nature, the establishment of

inventories of ecosystems and assessments of the effects on nature of proposed policies and activities; all of these elements shall be disclosed to the public by appropriate means in time to permit effective consultation and participation.

17. Funds, programmes and administrative structures necessary to achieve the objective of the conservation of nature shall be provided.

18. Constant efforts shall be made to increase knowledge of nature by scientific research and to disseminate such knowledge unimpeded by restrictions of any kind.

19. The status of natural processes, ecosystems and species shall be closely monitored to enable early detection of degradation or threat, ensure timely intervention and facilitate the evaluation of conservation policies and methods.

20. Military activities damaging to nature shall be avoided.

21. States and, to the extent they are able, other public authorities, international organizations, individuals, groups and corporations shall:

(a) Co-operate in the task of conserving nature through common activities and other relevant actions, including information exchange and consultations;

(b) Establish standards for products and manufacturing processes that may have adverse effects on nature, as well as agreed methodologies for assessing these effects;

(c) Implement the applicable international legal provisions for the conservation of nature and the protection of the environment;

(d) Ensure that activities within their jurisdiction or control do not cause damage to the natural systems located within other States or in the areas beyond the limits of national jurisdiction;

(e) Safeguard and conserve nature in areas beyond national jurisdiction.

22. Taking fully into account the sovereignty of States over their natural resources, each State shall give effect to the provisions of the present Charter through its competent organs and in co-operation with other States.

23. All persons, in accordance with their national legislation, shall have the opportunity to participate, individually or with others, in the formulation of decisions of direct concern to their environment, and shall have access to means of redress when their environment has suffered damage or degradation.

24. Each person has a duty to act in accordance with the provisions of the

present Charter; acting individually, in association with others or through participation in the political process, each person shall strive to ensure that the objectives and requirements of the present Charter are met.

OECD PRINCIPLES CONCERNING TRANSFRONTIER POLLUTION*

Paris, 14 November 1974

The Council

Considering that the protection and improvement of the environment are common objectives of Member countries;

Considering that the common interests of countries concerned by transfrontier pollution should induce them to co-operate more closely in a spirit of international solidarity and to initiate concerted action for preventing and controlling transfrontier pollution;

Having regard to the Recommendations of the United Nations Conference on the Human Environment held in Stockholm in June 1972 and in particular those Principles of the Declaration on the Human Environment which are relevant to transfrontier pollution;

On the proposal of the Environment Committee:

I. Recommends that, without prejudice to future developments in international law and international co-operation in relation to transfrontier pollution, Member countries should be guided in their environmental policy by the principles concerning transfrontier pollution contained in this Recommendation and its Annex, which is an integral part of this Recommendation.

II. Instructs the Environment Committee to prepare without delay taking account of the work undertaken by other international organisations, a programme of work designed to elaborate further these principles and to facilitate their practical implementation.

III. Recommends Member countries to co-operate in developing international law applicable to transfrontier pollution.

IV. Instructs the Environment Committee, within the framework of its mandate, to examine or investigate further, as the case may be, the issues

---

*OECD Council Recommendation C(74)224 adopted on 14 November 1974. In: OECD and the Environment (Paris: OECD, 1979) pp. 106–112.

related to the Principles of the Stockholm Declaration regarding responsibility and liability, taking into account the work undertaken by other international organisations, to submit a first report to the Council on its work by 1 March, 1976 and to seek to formulate as soon as possible Draft Recommendations.

V. Instructs the Environment Committee to investigate further the issues concerning equal right of hearing, to formulate as soon as possible Draft Recommendations and to report to the Council on its work by 1 July, 1975.

ANNEX

Some Principles concerning Transfrontier Pollution

Title A. Introduction

This Annex sets forth some principles designed to facilitate the development of harmonized environmental policies with a view to solving transfrontier pollution problems. Their implementation should be based on a fair balance of rights and obligations among countries concerned by transfrontier pollution.

These principles should subsequently be supplemented and developed in the light of work undertaken by the OECD or other appropriate international organisations.

For the purpose of these principles, pollution means the introduction by man, directly or indirectly, of substances or energy into the environment resulting in deleterious effects of such a nature as to endanger human health, harm living resources and ecosystems, and impair or interface with amenities and other legitimate uses of the environment.

Unless otherwise specified, these principles deal with pollution originating in one country and having effect within other countries.

Title B.[1] International solidarity

1. Countries should define a concerted long-term policy for the protection and improvement of the environment in zones liable to be affected by transfrontier pollution.

---

[1] The delegate for Spain reserved his position on Title B.

Without prejudice to their rights and obligations under international law and in accordance with their responsibility under Principle 21 of the Stockholm Declaration, countries should seek, as far as possible, an equitable balance of their rights and obligations as regards the zones concerned by transfrontier pollution.

In implementing this concerted policy, countries should among other things:

(a) take account of:

—levels of existing pollution and the present quality of the environment concerned;

—the nature and quantities of pollutants;

—the assimilative capacity of the environment, as established by mutual agreement by the countries concerned, taking into account the particular characteristics and use of the affected zone;

—activities at the source of pollution and activities and uses sensitive to such pollution;

—the situation, prospective use and development of the zones concerned from a socio-economic standpoint;

(b) define:

—environmental quality objectives and corresponding protective measures;

(c) promote:

—guidelines for a land-use planning policy consistent with the requirements both of environmental protection and socio-economic development;

(d) draw up and maintain up to date:

(i) list of particularly dangerous substances regarding which efforts should be made to eliminate polluting discharges, if necessary by stages, and

(ii) lists of substances regarding which polluting discharges should be subject to very strict control.

2. Pending the definition of such concerted long-term policies countries should, individually and jointly, take all appropriate measures to prevent and control transfrontier pollution, and harmonize as far as possible their relevant policies.

3. Countries should endeavour to prevent any increase in transfrontier pollution, including that stemming from new or additional substances and activities, and to reduce, and as far as possible eliminate any transfrontier pollution existing between them within time limits to be specified.

Title C. Principle of non-discrimination

4. Countries should initially base their action on the principle of non-discrimination, whereby:

(a) polluters causing transfrontier pollution should be subject to legal or statutory provisions no less severe than those which would apply for any equivalent pollution occurring within their country, under comparable conditions and in comparable zones, taking into account, when appropriate, the special nature and environmental needs of the zone affected;

(b) in particular, without prejudice to quality objectives or standards applying to transfrontier pollution mutually agreed upon by the countries concerned, the levels of transfrontier pollution entering into the zones liable to be affected by such pollution should not exceed those considered acceptable under comparable conditions and in comparable zones inside the country in which it originates, taking into account, when appropriate, the special state of the environment in the affected country;

(c) any country whenever it applies the Polluter-Pays Principle should apply it to all polluters within this country without making any difference according to whether pollution affects this country or another country;

(d) persons affected by transfrontier pollution should be granted no less favourable treatment than persons affected by a similar pollution in the country from which such transfrontier pollution originates.

Title D.[2] Principle of equal right of hearing

5. Countries should make every effort to introduce, where not already in existence, a system affording equal right of hearing, according to which:

(a) whenever a project, a new activity or a course of conduct may create a significant risk of transfrontier pollution and is investigated by public authorities, those who may be affected by such pollution should have the same rights of standing in judicial or administrative proceedings in the country where it originates as those of that country;

(b) whenever transfrontier pollution gives rise to damage in a country, those who are affected by such pollution should have the same rights of standing in judicial or administrative proceedings in the country where such pollution originates as those of that country, and they should be extended procedural rights equivalent to the rights extended to those of that country.

Title E.[3] Principle of information and consultation

6. Prior to the initiation in a country of works or undertakings which might create a significant risk of transfrontier pollution, this country should

---

[2] The delegate for Spain reserved his position on Title D.
[3] The delegate for Spain reserved his position on Title E.

provide early information to other countries which are or may be affected. It should provide these countries with relevant information and data, the transmission of which is not prohibited by legislative provisions or prescriptions or applicable international conventions, and should invite their comments.

7. Countries should enter into consultation on an existing or foreseeable transfrontier pollution problem at the request of a country which is or may be directly affected and should diligently pursue such consultations on this particular problem over a reasonable period of time.

8. Countries should refrain from carrying out projects or activities which might create a significant risk of transfrontier pollution without first informing the countries which are or may be affected and, except in cases of extreme urgency, providing a reasonable amount of time in the light of circumstances for diligent consultation. Such consultations held in the best spirit of co-operation and good neighbourliness should not enable a country to unreasonably delay or to impede the activities or projects on which consultations are taking place.

Title F. Warning systems and incidents

9. Countries should promptly warn other potentially affected countries of any situation which may cause any sudden increase in the level of pollution in areas outside the country of origin of pollution, and take all appropriate steps to reduce the effects of any such sudden increase.

10. Countries should assist each other, wherever necessary, in order to prevent incidents which may result in transfrontier pollution, and to minimize, and if possible eliminate, the effects of such incidents, and should develop contingency plans to this end.

Title G. Exchange of scientific information, monitoring measures and research

11. Countries concerned should exchange all relevant scientific information and data on transfrontier pollution, when not prohibited by legislative provisions or prescriptions or by applicable international conventions. They should develop and adopt pollution measurement methods providing results which are compatible.

12. They should, when appropriate, co-operate in scientific and technical research programmes inter alia for identifying the origin and pathways of transfrontier pollution, any damage caused and the best methods of pollution

prevention and control, and should share all information and data thus obtained.

They should, where necessary, consider setting up jointly, in zones affected by transfrontier pollution, a permanent monitoring system or network for assessing the levels of pollution and the effectiveness of measures taken by them to reduce pollution.

Title H. Institutions

13. Countries concerned by a particular problem of transfrontier pollution should consider the advantages of co-operation, by setting up international commissions or other bodies, or by strengthening existing institutions, in order to deal more effectively with particular aspects of such problems.

Such institutions could be authorized to collect any data needed for a proper evaluation of the problem and its causes, and make to the countries concerned practical proposals for concerted efforts to combat transfrontier pollution. With the consent of the States concerned, they could also carry out any necessary additional investigations into the origin and degree of pollution, review the effectiveness of any pollution prevention and control measures which have been taken, and publish reports of their findings.

Title I. Disputes

14. Should negotiations and other means of diplomatically settling disputes concerning transfrontier pollution fail, countries should have the opportunity to submit such a dispute to a procedure of legal settlement which is prompt, effective and binding.

Title J. International agreements

15. Countries should endeavour to conclude, where necessary, bilateral or multilateral agreements for the abatement of transfrontier pollution in accordance with the above principles, to bring promptly into force any agreements which may already have been signed.

16. When negotiating new bilateral or multilateral agreements countries should, while taking into account the principles set out above, strive for the application of efficient pollution prevention and control measures in accordance with the Polluter-Pays Principle.

Such agreements could, inter alia, include provisions for practical procedures promoting the prompt and equitable compensation of persons affected by transfrontier pollution, and could also contain procedures facilitating the provision of information and consultation.

IIL RESOLUTION ON THE USE OF INTERNATIONAL NON-MARITIME WATERS*

Salzbourg, 11 September 1961

The Institute of International Law

Considering that the economic value of the use of waters has been modified by modern techniques and that the application of said techniques to the waters of a river basin extending upon the territory of several States generally affects the whole of these States, and that this evolution requires an adjustment in the legal field;

Considering that there is a common interest in maximizing the use of available natural resources;

Considering that the obligation not to cause an unlawful prejudice to a third party is one of the basic principles governing general relations between neighbouring countries;

Considering that this principle also applies to relations deriving from the various uses of waters;

Considering that, for the use of waters involving several States, each of the above-mentioned States may obtain, through consultations, joint planning and reciprocal concessions, the benefits of a more efficient development of natural resources;

Notes the existence of the following rules in international law and makes the following recommendations:

Article I

The present rules and recommendations apply to the use of waters which are part of a river or of a watershed extending upon the territory of two or more States.

---

*In: Annuaire de l'Institut de droit international, Vol. 49-II, Salzbourg Session, September 1961, (Basle, 1961), pp. 381–384.

Article II

Every State has the right to make use of the waters flowing across or bordering its territory subject to the limitations imposed by international law and in particular those which result from the following legal dispositions. That right is limited by the right of use by the other States concerned with the same river or watershed.

Article III

If the various States disagree upon the extent of their rights of use, the disagreement shall be settled on the basis of equity, taking into consideration the respective needs of the States, as well as any other circumstances relevant to any particular case.

Article IV

Each State may only proceed with works or to use the waters of a river or watershed that may affect the possibilities of use of the same waters by other States on condition of preserving for those States the benefit of the advantages to which they are entitled by virtue of Article III, as well as adequate compensation for any losses or damages incurred.

Article V

The works or uses referred to in the abovementioned article may only be initiated after due advance notice has been given to the States concerned.

Article VI

If objections are raised, the States shall enter in negotiations in view of reaching an agreement within a reasonable time. To this end, it is desirable that the States involved make use of technical expertises and if need be of appropriate commissions and organizations to reach solutions ensuring maximum benefits for all concerned.

Article VII

During the negotiations, every State should, according to the principle of good faith, refrain from proceeding with the works or uses in dispute, or from taking any other measures likely to aggravate the conflict or to make a settlement more difficult.

Article VIII

If the States involved cannot reach an agreement within a reasonable time, it is recommended to submit to judicial or arbitral settlement the question whether the intended development runs counter to the abovementioned rules. If the State raising objections to the projected works or uses is opposed to any judicial or arbitral settlement, the other State remains free, under its own responsibility, to proceed with said works or uses, while remaining obligated by the provisions of Articles II to IV.

Article IX

It is recommended to the States concerned by particular watersheds to consider whether it would not be appropriate to set up joint organizations for the preparation of water utilization plans to facilitate their economic development, as well as to prevent or settle any disputes that might occur.

IIL RESOLUTION ON THE POLLUTION OF RIVERS AND LAKES AND INTERNATIONAL LAW*

Athens, 12 September 1979

The Institute of International Law

Recalling its Resolutions of Madrid in 1911 and of Salzbourg in 1961;

Conscious of the multiple potential uses of international rivers and lakes and of the common interest in a rational and equitable utilization of such resources through the achievement of a reasonable balance between the various interests;

Considering that pollution spread by rivers and lakes to the territories of more than one State is assuming increasingly alarming and diversified proportions whilst protection and improvement of the environment are duties incumbent upon States;

Recalling the obligation to respect the sovereignty of every State over its territory, as a result of which each State has the obligation to avoid any use of its own territory that causes injury in the territory of another State,

Hereby adopts the following articles:

Article I

1. For the purpose of this Resolution, "pollution" means any physical, chemical or biological alteration in the composition or quality of waters which results directly or indirectly from human action and affects the legitimate uses of such waters, thereby causing injury.

2. In specific cases, the existence of pollution and the characteristics thereof shall, to the extent possible, be determined by referring to environmental norms established through agreements or by the competent international organizations and commissions.

3. This Resolution shall apply to international rivers and lakes and to their basins.

---

*In: Annuaire de l'Institut de droit international, Vol. 58-I, Athens Session, September 1979 (Basle/Munich, 1980), p. 197 et seq. The reproduced text is a translation of the authentic French text.

Article II

In the exercise of their sovereign right to exploit their own resources pursuant to their own environmental policies, and without prejudice to their contractual obligations, States shall be under a duty to ensure that their activities or those conducted within their jurisdiction or under their control cause no pollution in the waters of international rivers and lakes beyond their boundaries.

Article III

1. For the purpose of fulfilling their obligation under Article II, States shall take, and adapt to the circumstances, all measures required to:

(a) prevent any new form of pollution or any increase in the existing degree of pollution; and

(b) abate existing pollution within the best possible time limits.

2. Such measures shall be particularly strict in the case of ultra-hazardous activities or activities which pose a danger to highly exposed areas or environments.

Article IV

In order to comply with the obligations set forth in articles II and III, States shall in particular use the following means:

(a) at national level, enactment of all necessary laws and regulations and adoption of efficient and adequate administrative measures and judicial procedures for the enforcement of such laws and regulations;

(b) at international level, cooperation in good faith with the other States concerned.

Article V

States shall incur international liability under international law for any breach of their international obligations with respect to pollution of rivers and lakes.

Article VI

With a view to ensuring an effective system of prevention and of compensation for victims of transboundary pollution, States should conclude international conventions concerning in particular:

(a) the jurisdiction of courts, the applicable law and the enforcement of judgements;

(b) the procedure for special arrangements providing in particular for objective liability systems and compensation funds with regard to pollution brought about by ultra-hazardous activities.

Article VII

1. In carrying out their duty to cooperate, States bordering the same hydrographic basin shall, as far as practicable, especially through agreements, resort to the following ways of cooperation:

(a) inform co-riparian States regularly of all appropriate data on the pollution of the basin, its causes, its nature, the damage resulting from it and the preventive procedures;

(b) notify the States concerned in due time of any activities envisaged in their own territories which may involve the basin in a significant threat of transboundary pollution;

(c) promptly inform States that might be affected by a sudden increase in the level of transboundary pollution in the basin and take all appropriate steps to reduce the effects of any such increase;

(d) consult with each other on actual or potential problems of transboundary pollution of the basin so as to reach, by methods of their own choice, a solution consistent with the interests of the States concerned and with the protection of the environment;

(e) coordinate or pool their scientific and technical research programmes to combat pollution of the basin;

(f) establish by common agreement environmental norms, in particular quality norms for the whole or part of the basin;

(g) set up international commissions with the largest terms of reference for the entire basin, providing for the participation of local authorities if this proves useful, or strengthen the powers or coordination of existing institutions;

(h) establish harmonized, coordinated or unified networks for permanent observation and pollution control;

(i) develop safeguards for individuals who may be affected by polluting activities, both at the stages of prevention and compensation, by granting on a non-discriminatory basis the greatest access to judicial and administrative procedures in States in which such activities originate and by setting up compensation funds for ecological damage the origin of which cannot be clearly determined or which is of exceptional magnitude.

Article VIII

In order to assist developing States in the fulfilment of the obligations and in the implementation of the recommendation referred to in this Resolution, it is desirable that developed States and competent international organizations provide such States with technical assistance or any other assistance as may be appropriate in this field.

Article IX

This Resolution is without prejudice to the obligations which fundamental human rights impose upon States with regard to pollution occurring in their own territories.

ILA HELSINKI RULES ON THE USES OF THE WATERS OF INTERNATIONAL RIVERS*

Helsinki, 20 August 1966

Chapter 1—General

Article I

The general rules of international law as set forth in these chapters are applicable to the use of the waters of an international drainage basin except as may be provided otherwise by convention, agreement or binding custom among the basin States.

Article II

An international drainage basin is a geographical area extending over two or more States determined by the watershed limits of the system of waters, including surface and underground waters, flowing into a common terminus.

Article III

A "basin State" is a state the territory of which includes a portion of an international drainage basin.

Chapter 2—Equitable Utilization of the Waters of an International Drainage Basin

Article IV

Each basin State is entitled, within its territory, to a reasonable and equitable share in the beneficial uses of the waters of an international drainage basin.

---

*In: The International Law Association, Report of the Fifty-Second Conference, Helsinki, 14–20 August, 1966 (London, 1967), pp. 484–532.

Article V

1. What is a reasonable and equitable share within the meaning of Article IV is to be determined in the light of all the relevant factors in each particular case.

2. Relevant factors which are to be considered include, but are not limited to:

(a) the geography of the basin, including in particular the extent of the drainage area in the territory of each basin State;

(b) the hydrology of the basin, including in particular the contribution of water by each basin State;

(c) the climate affecting the basin;

(d) the past utilization of the waters of the basin, including in particular existing utilization;

(e) the economic and social needs of each basin State;

(f) the population dependent on the waters of the basin in each basin State;

(g) the comparative costs of alternative means of satisfying the economic and social needs of each basin State;

(h) the availability of other resources;

(i) the avoidance of unnecessary waste in the utilization of waters of the basin;

(j) the practicability of compensation to one or more of the co-basin States as a means of adjusting conflicts among uses; and,

(k) the degree to which the needs of a basin State may be satisfied, without causing substantial injury to a co-basin State.

3. The weight to be given to each factor is to be determined by its importance in comparison with that of other relevant factors. In determining what is a reasonable and equitable share, all relevant factors are to be considered together and a conclusion reached on the basis of the whole.

Article VI

A use or category of uses is not entitled to any inherent preference over any other use or category of uses.

Article VII

A basin State may not be denied the present reasonable use of the waters of an international drainage basin to reserve for a co-basin State a future use of such waters.

Article VIII

1. An existing reasonable use may continue in operation unless the factors justifying its continuance are outweighed by other factors leading to the conclusion that it be modified or terminated so as to accommodate a competing incompatible use.

2. (a) A use that is in fact in operation is deemed to have been an existing use from the time of the initiation of construction directly related to the use or, where such construction is not required, the undertaking of comparable acts of actual implementation.

(b) Such a use continues to be an existing use until such time as it is discontinued with the intention that it be abandoned.

3. A use will not be deemed an existing use if at the time of becoming operational it is incompatible with an already existing reasonable use.

Chapter 3—Pollution

Article IX

As used in this Chapter, the term "water pollution" refers to any detrimental change resulting from human conduct in the natural composition, content, or quality of the waters of an international drainage basin.

Article X

1. Consistent with the principle of equitable utilization of the waters of an international drainage basin, a State:

(a) must prevent any new form of water pollution or any increase in the degree of existing water pollution in an international drainage basin which would cause substantial injury in the territory of a co-basin State, and

(b) should take all reasonable measures to abate existing water pollution in an international drainage basin to such an extent that no substantial damage is caused in the territory of a co-basin State.

2. The rule stated in paragraph (1) of this Article applies to water pollution originating:

(a) within a territory of the State, or

(b) outside the territory of the State, if it is caused by the State's conduct.

Article XI

1. In the case of a violation of the rule stated in paragraph (1)a. of Article X of this Chapter, the State responsible shall be required to cease the wrongful conduct and compensate the injured co-basin State for the injury that has been caused to it.

2. In a case falling under the rule stated in paragraph (1)b. of Article X, if a State fails to take reasonable measures, it shall be required promptly to enter into negotiations with the injured State with a view toward reaching a settlement equitable under the circumstances.

Chapter 4—Navigation

Article XII

1. This Chapter refers to those rivers and lakes portions of which are both navigable and separate or traverse the territories of two or more states.

2. Rivers or lakes are "navigable" if in their natural or canalized state they are currently used for commercial navigation or are capable by reason of their natural condition of being so used.

3. In this Chapter the term "riparian State" refers to a State through or along which the navigable portion of a river flows or a lake lies.

Article XIII

Subject to any limitations or qualifications referred to in these Chapters, each riparian State is entitled to enjoy rights of free navigation on the entire course of a river or lake.

Article XIV

"Free navigation", as the term is used in this Chapter, includes the following freedom for vessels of a riparian State on a basis of equality:

(a) freedom of movement on the entire navigable course of the river or lake;

(b) freedom to enter ports and to make use of plants and docks; and,

(c) freedom to transport goods and passengers, either directly or through transhipment, between the territory of one riparian State and the territory of another riparian State and between the territory of a riparian State and the open sea.

Article XV

A riparian State may exercise rights of police, including but not limited to the protection of public safety and health, over that portion of the river or lake subject to its jurisdiction, provided the exercise of such rights does not unreasonably interfere with the enjoyment of the rights of free navigation defined in Articles XIII and XIV.

Article XVI

Each riparian State may restrict or prohibit the loading by vessels of a foreign State of goods and passengers in its territory for discharge in such territory.

Article XVII

A riparian State may grant rights of navigation to non-riparian States on rivers or lakes within its territory.

Article XVIII

Each riparian State is, to the extent of the means available or made available to it, required to maintain in good order that portion of the navigable course of a river or lake within its jurisdiction.

Article XVIII bis[1]

1. A riparian State intending to undertake works to improve the navigability of that portion of a river or lake within its jurisdiction is under a duty to give notice to the co-riparian States.

2. If these works are likely to affect adversely the navigational uses of one

---

[1] Approved by the Fifty-Sixth Conference of the International Law Association, New Delhi, 1974. Text in: Report of the Committee on International Water Resources Law of the International Law Association, in: The International Law Association, Report of the Fifty-Sixth Conference, p. 15.

or more co-riparian States, any such co-riparian State may, within a reasonable time, request consultation. The concerned co-riparian States are then under a duty to negotiate.

3. If a riparian State proposes that such works be undertaken in whole or in part in the territory of one or more other co-riparian States, it must obtain the consent of the other co-riparian State or States concerned. The co-riparian State or States from whom this consent is required are under a duty to negotiate.

Article XIX

The rules stated in this Chapter are not applicable to the navigation of vessels of war or of vessels performing police or administrative functions, or, in general, exercising any other form of public authority.

Article XX

In time of war, other armed conflict, or public emergency constituting a threat to the life of the State, a riparian State may take measures derogating from its obligations under this Chapter to the extent strictly required by the exigencies of the situation, provided that such measures are not inconsistent with its other obligations under international law. The riparian State shall in any case facilitate navigation for humanitarian purposes.

Chapter 5—Timber Floating

Article XXI

The floating of timber on a watercourse which flows through or between the territories of two or more States is governed by the following Articles except in cases in which floating is governed by rules of navigation according to applicable law or custom binding upon the riparians.

Article XXII

The States riparian to an international watercourse utilized for navigation may determine by common consent whether and under what conditions timber floating may be permitted upon the watercourse.

Article XXIII

1. It is recommended that each State riparian to an international watercourse not used for navigation should, with due regard to other uses of the watercourse, authorize the co-riparian States to use the watercourse and its banks within the territory of each riparian State for the floating of timber.
2. This authorization should extend to all necessary work along the banks by the floating crew and to the installation of such facilities as may be required for the timber floating.

Article XXIV

If a riparian State requires permanent installation for floating inside a territory of a co-riparian State or if it is necessary to regulate the flow of the watercourse, all questions connected with these installations and measures should be determined by agreement between the States concerned.

Article XXV

Co-riparian States of a watercourse which is, or is to be used for floating timber should negotiate in order to come to an agreement governing the administrative regime of floating, and if necessary to establish a joint agency or commission in order to facilitate the regulation of floating in all aspects.

Chapter 6—Procedures for the Prevention and Settlement of Disputes

Article XXVI

This Chapter relates to procedures for the prevention and settlement of international disputes as to the legal rights or other interests of basin States and of other States in the waters of an international drainage basin.

Article XXVII

1. Consistently with the Charter of the United Nations, States are under an obligation to settle international disputes as to their legal rights or other interests by peaceful means in such a manner that international peace and security, and justice are not endangered.

2. It is recommended that States resort progressively to the means of prevention and settlement of disputes stipulated in Articles XXIX to XXXIV of this Chapter.

Article XXVIII

1. States are under a primary obligation to resort to means of prevention and settlement of disputes stipulated in the applicable treaties binding upon them.

2. States are limited to the means of prevention and settlement of disputes stipulated in treaties binding upon them only to the extent provided by the applicable treaties.

Article XXIX

1. With a view to preventing disputes from arising between basin States as to their legal rights or other interest, it is recommended that each basin State furnish relevant and reasonably available information to the other basin States concerning the waters of a drainage basin within its territory and its use of, and activities with respect to such waters.

2. A State, regardless of its location in a drainage basin, should in particular furnish to any other basin State, the interests of which may be substantially affected, notice of any proposed construction or installation which would alter the regime of the basin in a way which might give rise to a dispute as defined in Article XXVI. The notice should include such essential facts as will permit the recipient to make an assessment of the probable effect of the proposed alteration.

3. A State providing the notice referred to in paragraph (2) of this Article should afford to the recipient a reasonable period of time to make an assessment of the probable effect of the proposed construction or installation and to submit its views thereon to the State furnishing the notice.

4. If a State has failed to give the notice referred to in paragraph (2) of this Article, the alteration by the State in the regime of the drainage basin shall not be given the weight normally accorded to temporal priority in use in the event of a determination of what is a reasonable and equitable share of the waters of the basin.

Article XXX

In case of a dispute between States as to their legal rights or other interests, as defined in Article XXVI, they should seek a solution by negotiation.

Article XXXI

1. If a question or dispute arises which relates to the present or future utilization of the waters of an international drainage basin, it is recommended that the basin States refer the question or dispute to a joint agency and that they request the agency to survey the international drainage basin and to formulate plans or recommendations for the fullest and most efficient use thereof in the interests of all such States.

2. It is recommended that the joint agency be instructed to submit reports on all matters within its competence to the appropriate authorities of the member States concerned.

3. It is recommended that the member States of the joint agency in appropriate cases invite non-basin States which by treaty enjoy a right in the use of the waters of an international drainage basin to associate themselves with the work of the joint agency or that they be permitted to appear before the agency.

Article XXXII

If a question or a dispute is one which is considered by the States concerned to be incapable of resolution in the manner set forth in Article XXXI, it is recommended that they seek the good offices, or jointly request the mediation of a third State, of a qualified international organization or of a qualified person.

Article XXXIII

1. If the States concerned have not been able to resolve their dispute through negotiations or have been unable to agree on the measures described in Article XXXI and XXXII, it is recommended that they form a commission of inquiry or an ad hoc conciliation commission, which shall endeavour to find a solution, likely to be accepted by the States concerned, of any dispute as to their legal rights.

2. It is recommended that the conciliation commission be constituted in the manner set forth in the Annex.

Article XXXIV

It is recommended that the States concerned agree to submit their legal disputes to an ad hoc arbitral tribunal, to a permanent arbitral tribunal or to the International Court of Justice if:

(a) A commission has not been formed as provided in Article XXXIII, or

(b) The commission has not been able to find a solution to be recommended, or

(c) A solution recommended has not been accepted by the States concerned, and

(d) An agreement has not been otherwise arrived at.

Article XXXV

It is recommended that in the event of arbitration the States concerned have recourse to the Model Rules on Arbitral Procedure prepared by the International Law Commission of the United Nations at its tenth session in 1958.

Article XXXVI

Recourse to arbitration implies the undertaking by the States concerned to consider the award to be given as final and to submit in good faith to its execution.

Article XXXVII

The means of settlement referred to in the preceding Articles of this Chapter are without prejudice to the utilization of means of settlement recommended to, or required of, members of regional arrangements or agencies and of other international organizations.

Annex

Model Rules for the Constitution of the Conciliation Commission for the Settlement of a Dispute
(In implementation of Article XXXIII of Chapter 6)

Article I

The members of the Commission, including the President, shall be appointed by the States concerned.

Article II

If the States concerned cannot agree on these appointments, each State shall appoint two members. The members thus appointed shall choose one more member who shall be the President of the Commission. If the appointed members do not agree, the member-president shall be appointed, at the request of any State concerned, by the President of the International Court of Justice, or, if he does not make the appointment, by the Secretary-General of the United Nations.

Article III

The membership of the Commission should include persons who, by reason of their special competence, are qualified to deal with disputes concerning international drainage basins.

Article IV

If a member of the Commission abstains from performing his office or is unable to discharge his responsibilities, he shall be replaced by the procedure set out in Article I or Article II of this Annex, according to the manner in which he was originally appointed. If, in the case of:

1. a member originally appointed under Article I, the States fail to agree as to a replacement; or

2. a member originally appointed under Article II, the State involved fails to replace the member;

a replacement shall be chosen, at the request of any State concerned, by the President of the International Court of Justice, or, if he does not choose the replacement, by the Secretary-General of the United Nations.

Article V

In the absence of agreement to the contrary between the parties, the Conciliation Commission shall determine the place of its meetings and shall lay down its own procedure.

ILA MONTREAL RULES OF INTERNATIONAL LAW APPLICABLE TO TRANSFRONTIER POLLUTION*

Montreal, 4 September 1982

Article 1 (Applicability)

The following rules of international law concerning transfrontier pollution are applicable except as may be otherwise provided by convention, agreement or binding custom among the States concerned.

Article 2 (Definition)

1. "Pollution" means any introduction by man, directly or indirectly, of substance or energy into the environment resulting in deleterious effects of such a nature as to endanger human health, harm living resources, ecosystems and material property and impair amenities or interfere with other legitimate uses of the environment.

2. "Transfrontier pollution" means pollution of which the physical origin is wholly or in part situated within the territory of one State and which has deleterious effects in the territory of another State.

Article 3 (Prevention and Abatement)

1. Without prejudice to the operation of the rules relating to the reasonable and equitable utilisation of shared natural resources States are in their legitimate activities under an obligation to prevent, abate and control transfrontier pollution to such an extent that no substantial injury is caused in the territory of another State.

2. Furthermore States shall limit new and increased transfrontier pollution to the lowest level that may be reached by measures practicable and reasonable under the circumstances.

3. States should endeavour to reduce existing transfrontier pollution, below the requirements of paragraph 1 of this Article, to the lowest level that

---

*In: The International Law Association, Report of the Sixtieth Conference (Montreal, 1982) pp. 1–3.

may be reached by measures practicable and reasonable under the circumstances.

Article 4 (Highly Dangerous Substances)

Notwithstanding the provisions in Article 3 States shall refrain from causing transfrontier pollution by discharging into the environment substances generally considered as being highly dangerous to human health. If such substances are already being discharged, States shall eliminate the polluting discharge within a reasonable time.

Article 5 (Prior Notice)

1. States planning to carry out activities which might entail a significant risk of transfrontier pollution shall give early notice to States likely to be affected. In particular they shall on their own initiative or upon request of the potentially affected States, communicate such pertinent information as will permit the recipient to make an assessment of the probable effects of the planned activities.

2. In order to appraise whether a planned activity implies a significant risk of transfrontier pollution, States should make environmental assessment before carrying out such activities.

Article 6 (Consultations)

Upon request of a potentially affected State, the State furnishing the information shall enter into consultations on transfrontier pollution problems connected with the planned activities and pursue such consultations in good faith and over a reasonable period of time.

Article 7 (Emergency Situations)

When as a result of an emergency situation or of other circumstances activities already carried out in the territory of a state cause or might cause a sudden increase in the existing level of transfrontier pollution the State of origin is under a duty:

(a) to promptly warn the affected or potentially affected States;

(b) to provide them with such pertinent information as will enable them to minimize the transfrontier pollution damage;

(c) to inform them of the steps taken to abate the cause of the increased transfrontier pollution level.

ILA MONTREAL RULES ON WATER POLLUTION IN AN INTERNATIONAL DRAINAGE BASIN*

Montreal, 4 September 1982

Article 1

Consistent with the Helsinki Rules on the equitable utilization of the waters on an international drainage basin, States shall ensure that activities conducted within their territory or under their control conform with the principles set forth in these Articles concerning water pollution in an international drainage basin. In particular, States shall:

(a) prevent new or increased water pollution that would cause substantial injury in the territory of another State;

(b) take all reasonable measures to abate existing water pollution to such an extent that no substantial injury is caused in the territory of another State; and

(c) attempt to further reduce any such water pollution to the lowest level that is practicable and reasonable under the circumstances.

Article 2

Notwithstanding the provision of Article 1, States shall not discharge or permit the discharge of substances generally considered to be highly dangerous into the waters of an international drainage basin.

Article 3

In order to give effect to Articles 1 and 2 above, States shall enact all necessary laws and regulations and adopt efficient and adequate administrative measures and judicial procedures for the enforcement of these laws and regulations.

Article 4

In order to give effect to the provisions of these Articles, States shall co-operate with the other States concerned.

---

*In: The International Law Association, Report of the Sixtieth Conference (Montreal, 1982) pp. 13, 535 et seq.

Article 5

Basin States shall:

(a) inform the other States concerned regularly of all relevant and reasonably available data, both qualitative and quantitative, on the pollution of waters of the basin, its causes, its nature, the damage resulting from it, and the preventive procedures;

(b) notify the other States concerned in due time of any activities envisaged in their own territories that may involve a significant threat of, or increase in, water pollution in the territories of those other States; and

(c) promptly inform States that might be affected, of any sudden change of circumstances that may cause or increase water pollution in the territories of those other States.

Article 6

Basin States shall consult one another on actual or potential problems of water pollution in the drainage basin so as to reach, by methods of their own choice, a solution consistent with their rights and duties under international law. This consultation, however, shall not unreasonably delay the implementation of plans that are the subject of the consultation.

Article 7

In order to ensure an effective system of prevention and abatement of water pollution of an international drainage basin, basin States should set up appropriate international administrative machinery for the entire basin. In any event, they should:

(a) co-ordinate or pool their scientific and technical research programmes to combat water pollution;

(b) establish harmonized, co-ordinated, or unified networks for permanent observation and pollution control; and

(c) establish jointly water quality objectives and standards for the whole or part of the basin.

Article 8

States should provide remedies for persons who are or may be adversely affected by water pollution in an international drainage basin. In particular, States should, on a non-discriminatory basis, grant these persons access to the judicial and administrative agencies of the State in whose territory the pollution originates, and should provide, by agreement or otherwise, for such matters as the jurisdiction of courts, the applicable law, and the enforcement of judgments.

Article 9

In the case of a breach of a State's international obligations relating to water pollution in an international drainage basin, that State shall cease the wrongful conduct and shall pay compensation for the injury resulting therefrom.

Article 10

When it is contended that the conduct of a State is not in accordance with its obligations under these Articles, that State shall promptly enter into negotiations with the complaining State with a view of reaching a solution that is equitable under the circumstances.

Article 11

In the case of a dispute concerning water pollution in an international drainage basin, Articles XXXI to XXXVII of the Helsinki Rules shall, as far as possible, be applicable.

ANNEX II

MANDATE OF THE WORLD COMMISSION ON ENVIRONMENT AND DEVELOPMENT*

The World Commission on Environment and Development has been established at a time of unprecedented growth in pressures on the global environment, with grave predictions about the human future becoming commonplace.

The Commission is confident that it is possible to build a future that is more prosperous, more just, and more secure because it rests on policies and practices that serve to expand and sustain the ecological basis of development.

The Commission is convinced, however, that this will not happen without significant changes in current approaches: changes in perspectives, attitudes and life styles; changes in certain critical policies and the ways in which they are formulated and applied; changes in the nature of co-operation between governments, business, science and people; changes in certain forms of international co-operation which have proved incapable of tackling many environment and development issues; changes, above all, in the level of understanding and commitment by people, organizations and governments.

The World Commission on Environment and Development therefore invites suggestions, participation and support in order to assist it urgently:

(i) to re-examine the critical issues of environment and development and to formulate innovative, concrete and realistic action proposals to deal with them;

(ii) to strengthen international co-operation on environment and development and to assess and propose new forms of co-operation that can break out of existing patterns and influence policies and events in the direction of needed change; and

(iii) to raise the level of understanding and commitment to action on the part of individuals, voluntary organizations, businesses, institutes and governments.

---

*Adopted by the Commission at its Inaugural Meeting, Geneva, 1–3 October 1984.

ANNEX III

MEMBERS
OF THE WORLD COMMISSION
ON ENVIRONMENT AND DEVELOPMENT*

DR. GRO HARLEM BRUNDTLAND
(Chairman)
Former Prime Minister, present
Leader of the Opposition
Norway

DR. MANSOUR KHALID
(Vice Chairman)
Former Minister of Foreign Affairs
Sudan

MRS. SUSANNA AGNELLI
Under-Secretary of State
Ministry of Foreign Affairs
Italy

DR. SALEH AL-ATHEL
Executive Director and
Chairman of the Board of the
National Centre for Science
and Technology
Saudi Arabia

H.E. MR. BERNARD CHIDZERO
Minister of Finance, Economic
Planning and Development
Zimbabwe

H.E. MR. LAMINE MOHAMMED
FADIKA
Minister of Marine Affairs
Chairman of the National Council
for Environment
Ivory Coast

---

*As on 1 January 1985.

194

PROF. PABLO GONZALEZ
CASANOVA
Professor of Political and
Social Sciences
Institute for Political and
Social Studies
Mexico

DR. VOLKER HAUFF
Member of Parliament
Federal Republic of Germany

PROF. ISTVAN LANG
Secretary General
Hungarian Academy of Sciences
Hungary

DR. MA SHIJUN
Director
Research Centre of Ecology
Academia Sinica
People's Republic of China

MRS. MARGARITA MARINO
DE BOTERO
Director General
National Institute of Renewable
Natural Resources and the
Environment (INDERENA)
Colombia

H.E. JUDGE NAGENDRA SINGH
President of the International
Court of Justice
India

DR. PAULO NOGUEIRA-NETO
Secretary for Environment
Special Secretariat for
the Environment
Ministry of Urban Development
and Environment
Brazil

H.E. DR. SABURO OKITA
Former Minister of
Foreign Affairs
Chairman of the Institute for
Domestic and International
Policy Studies
Japan

MR. SHRIDATH S. RAMPHAL
Secretary General of the
Commonwealth Secretariat
Guyana

MR. WILLIAM D. RUCKELSHAUS
Attorney
Law firm of Perkins Coie
United States of America

H.E. MR. MOHAMED SAHNOUN
Ambassador to the United States
of America
Algeria

H.E. EMIL SALIM
Minister of State for
Population and Environment
Indonesia

H.E. MR. BUKAR SHAIB
Federal Minister of Agriculture
Water Resources and Rural
Development
Nigeria

ACADEMICIAN VLADIMIR
E. SOKOLOV
Member of the Presidium
of the Academy of Sciences
USSR

MR. JANEZ STANOVNIK
Member of the Presidency of the
Socialist Republic of Slovenia
Yugoslavia

MR. MAURICE F. STRONG
Executive Co-ordinator
United Nations Office for
Emergency Operations in Africa
Canada

EX OFFICIO

MR. JIM MACNEILL
Secretary-General of the Commission
Canada